Creating Value Through Project-Based Supply Chain Decisions

Creating Value Through Project-Based Supply Chain Decisions

Denise Chenger

BEP

BUSINESS EXPERT PRESS

Leader in applied, concise business books

Creating Value Through Project-Based Supply Chain Decisions

First published in 2024 by
Business Expert Press, LLC
222 East 46th Street, New York, NY 10017
www.businessexpertpress.com

ISBN-13: 978-1-63742-722-4 (paperback)
ISBN-13: 978-1-63742-723-1 (e-book)

Business Expert Press Portfolio and Project Management Collection

First edition: 2024

10 9 8 7 6 5 4 3 2 1

Dad—for the laughter, and always, without fail, finding something good in every person you met

Description

Good project decisions result in successful careers and profitable companies. Bad decisions can be costly, cause operational downtime, may hurt employee morale, and impact customers and suppliers. Making a good decision has become very difficult because of increasing operating complexity and less marketplace predictability. Because of this, employers rate critical thinking and decision making as a top essential skill.

Business problems are complex—so why do we continue to use a standard one-dimensional approach to solve complex, risky, and unpredictable problems?

This book takes a novel but practical, multi dimensional approach to making value-creating project decisions–decisions which use fewer resources to produce maximum value, including:

- Link company strategy and goals to project concepts
- How to assess which projects produce value
- Risk
- Make-or-buy project criteria
- Service-based project decisions

This book is intended for project managers, supply chain professionals, and operationally focused roles for individuals having responsibility for successfully delivering projects and wanting to take charge of their career.

Contents

Preface

If we keep using a one-dimensional approach to solve complex, multi-dimensional problems, we can't expect that much will change.

—**Denise Chenger**

There is a LOT going on in this book. Maybe too much. I will leave that judgment up to you, the reader. However, the world is ever-changing, and business is moving faster. We need to start thinking differently about the problems we are faced with and the approach used to tackle them. Continuing to take a one-dimensional approach through the lens of just one discipline can only provide a certain level of success—we are only seeing the problem through a very narrow lens. What's more, this approach continues to reinforce a siloed approach to business.

But what if we take a multi dimensional approach to business problems and opportunities? Doesn't this allow us to cross boundaries and expand our mind to think about things a little differently? Could it instill more empathy and understanding for the challenges faced by other functions and give us new perspectives for points of agreement and alignment? Might this approach promote more creativity and innovation?

This approach has always served me well. … Well, that's not entirely true, or at least it doesn't tell the whole story. Let's step back for a minute. Earlier in my career, recruiters would look at my resume and say "Wow! You have done a lot of interesting things but I am unclear on exactly what it is you can do for us? Where exactly would I place you?" It was up to me to sell my capabilities. Over the last two decades, this viewpoint has shifted. Today, there is research to support that gaining diverse experience from a variety of domains is more valuable in our fast-moving economy. Further, having a broader range of opportunities along with exposure across functions will build a more diverse foundation on which to make connections for decision making. Perhaps, more importantly, there is evidence supporting that diverse experience correlates with a higher salary.

So how might you, the reader, use this book and what will you gain by doing so? The intent is to help project managers and supply chain professionals in the early stages of their careers by providing a good foundation for making value-creating project decisions. However, I also see value for anyone who is thinking about initiating a project aimed at creating value in their company.

Projects embody strategy: a project must reflect how the business intends to drive value. Therefore, we must understand our company strategy and vision, how functions interact together in the value chain to create value, the business processes for getting work done, and how we assess risk and opportunity. This is required so that our decisions are aligned with our company's; needed in order to drive value. Therefore, I suggest each of us, regardless of what position or role we have in our company, has to think a little differently and learn a little more about how our company operates to create that value. But before we can do this, we need to understand a little more on what a decision is, how we make them, and how they relate to creating (or destroying) value in our project decisions.

I hope you join me on this journey aimed at thinking about our project decisions and our company's a little differently while diversifying our own competencies.

Acknowledgments

First, to Dr. Francis Hartman, who was my PhD supervisor. Dr. Hartman was a non conventional thinker and did not conform to a traditional perspective of project management; exactly what I needed. You never failed to challenge my thinking and helped me to see both project management and business under a new lens. In an effort to understand the complexities surrounding projects, you endorsed my desire to study the topic from a multi-dimensional and multi-disciplinary approach. While your book set the standard, I humbly make my own attempt. Second, to Dr. Kam Juddev, who planted this seed and has continued to provide constructive suggestions, mentorship, and guidance along the way. Next, to Dr. Jaana Woiceshyn, who set the bar high and pushed me to achieve what always initially felt like the impossible, while always giving me a safe place to land. And finally, to my colleagues Adi, Rajbir, Christian, and Leah, who provided feedback and encouragement with the book.

To my students, who were sponges with what I threw at them and almost always, without fail, gave me back more with their creative, inspirational, and generally cool stuff. I learned a ton from you all. I hope you carry on the journey we started and make some real, positive changes out in the big, exciting world.

To my amazing friends and family, who supported me through my academic career. No one will be happier that this book is published than each of you. Thank you. To my sister: you are a pillar of strength and you never fail to support me and listen to me with all of my crazy ideas, and for always answering "how did I get here?"

Finally, to my partner Rob – my north star. My rock. You helped me shift my priorities and supported me through the process. I look forward to many new and great adventures together!

PART 1

Building a Foundation for Making Value-Creating Supply Chain Project Decisions

CHAPTER 1

Introduction to Project Decisions

Introduction to Supply Chain Projects

Its a fact: the pace of business moves faster every year, and there is no expectation that the pace will slow down. This is, in part, due to globalization, which has been increasing over the last 20 years. Technology has enabled this trend. Before the 2000s, a small business would have considered its customers and competitors to be located near its own business. Today, that same small business competes with those same local companies but it may also be competing in a global market. Globalization has opened the door for a small business to source its goods and services globally and potentially at more competitive prices. It has become commonplace for a business in one country to forge relationships with other suppliers and customers around the globe. For consumers, technology provides a platform to find an obscure small business almost anywhere in the world. This trend suggests that our supply chains have radically shifted over the last couple of decades.

Globalization and technology have enabled both businesses and consumers to take more control and ownership of their sourcing (the process of finding and assessing suppliers) and purchasing decisions. For example, before 2000, it was almost impossible to make travel arrangements without the aid of a travel agency. As a consumer, we had to first locate a travel agency (often through the "yellow pages") that specialized in the geography of where we wanted to travel. And for an agent to know about and specialize in a particular geography, it meant that the agent probably had taken a trip there. Once the agent had the clients' request, the agent would take a week or more to put together a package that included hotels, tours, and airline tickets. It was difficult, if not impossible, for a consumer to book out-of-country trips without the help of a travel agent. Contrast this example with today: most people can locate hotels, source local activities, and educate themselves about travel information from their own home in minutes. In addition, currency exchange rates, required vaccines, or other information can easily be found without the help of a third party. Trips can be booked, confirmed, changed, or canceled without using the yellow pages, a travel agent, or any other middleperson. Essentially, as consumers, we have each participated in globalization and therefore influenced the redesigning of global supply chains. This simple example helps us define what a supply chain is: the resources and processes required to produce and sell a product or service from raw materials through to the customer.[1] This book is intended for the professionals making supply chain project decisions.

In a symbiotic relationship, globalization, along with technology, has enabled efficiencies for both small and large businesses. However, it has also made for a strongly competitive marketplace where businesses must continually look for opportunities to reduce costs and/or add value in order to remain relevant to their customers. Value can be added by improving or developing new products and services for customers. It has become necessary to work closely with supply chain partners or search for new partnerships to help enhance our business proposition. Tapping into our supply chains to look for efficiencies has become commonplace.

Global issues such as COVID-19 demonstrate the importance of supply chain relationships and the fragility of the threads linking a company to its broader supply chain network. Issues such as environmental, social, and corporate governance (ESG) factors have also impacted supply chains. Because of this, knowledge about where products and services originate, the materials used, and how they are produced has become relevant to most consumers (many consumers wish to make purchasing decisions aligned with their own values). Therefore, companies must be vigilant and transparent with their supply chain practices and ensure that those practices align with their corporate goals and identity. For example, a company stating that they are reducing their carbon footprint should demonstrate how they're doing it.

While many definitions of supply chain management exist, the following is used in this book "the systemic, strategic coordination of the traditional business functions and the tactics across these business functions within a particular company and across businesses within the supply chain, for the purposes of improving the long-term performance of the individual companies and the supply chain as a whole."[2]

Although supply chains have been altered and perhaps streamlined over the last couple of decades, supply chain management remains a complex endeavor and involves intra- and inter-company. Employees are expected to seek out and manage supply chain partnerships that are aligned with their company goals and identity while, working to create operational efficiencies. Employees then seek customer feedback and monitor changing customer needs.

Today, many companies have a dedicated supply chain function using professionals who can help lead and manage supply chain activities. While a supply chain professional will work in tandem with operations staff, their role is to lead the process of sourcing a new supplier, negotiating contracts, and managing the ongoing supplier relationship. Most companies rely on the supply chain team to design and execute supply chain decisions that are aligned with company goals and strategy.

Other responsibilities of supply chain professionals include seeking out changes by regulatory and government bodies to ensure compliance. They seek information about the competitive environment in which their suppliers operate, and they provide relevant information to their internal customers. In exchange, the role of these internal customers is to provide the supply chain partner with relevant information about their customers and the environment in which a function (the term used in this book versus a department) operates. This is required as it is no longer possible for a company to survive operating in isolation, without relationships that extend beyond the company's boundary.[3] Strong relationships, both inter- and intra-firm, aim to ensure that all employees are aware of issues associated with the competitive landscape that their company operates within. This serves to speed up decision making when required and produces the ability to pivot quicker. Relevant and current information helps ensure that small problems can be resolved quickly before growing into major issues. For example, resolving a supplier issue prior to incurring an interruption in operations or manufacturing will prevent customer impacts while ensuring the profitability and reputation of the company remain intact.

Supply chain professionals, employing relevant decision making processes and resources, have access to real-time information, and they are adept at making value-creating decisions that can be relied upon to address potential problems or issues and to take appropriate action to avoid major disruptions in company operations. Value-creating decisions expend a minimal number of resources, are done in an efficient manner, and create opportunities, revenue, and ultimately profit for a company. Note that any decision must adhere to all regulatory, safety, quality, or other lawful requirements and be ethical (refer to Chapter 8). Employees who can make these decisions are usually treasured at their company.

Regardless of whether you are a supply chain professional or have some other role within a company, learning how to make a decision is often absent from our workplace training or formal academic education. Postsecondary education equips us with theoretical knowledge we can use to make a decision, but it doesn't teach us *how* to make a *good* decision. Students gain practical experience in how to apply that knowledge to assignments and case studies submitted to instructors. The instructors may provide meaningful feedback on academic projects that can help gauge learning and application of theory. Students may also participate in the workplace through summer work terms or cooperative opportunities. In these capacities, students are given the opportunity to produce projects for their employer. However, until a person holds responsibility and accountability for decision making as an employee, it is difficult to accurately gauge whether a student, or employee, is making a good decision. It is important to note that many decisions will appear to be good decisions if they are evaluated in the short term. However, it is particularly important to track a decision over an extended, specific period. For example, only over a specific time period can a company track savings associated with a decision or increased customer retention, or monitor the quality of products purchased from a new supplier.

The intent of this book is not just to learn how to make decisions, but rather, value-creating decisions. Value-creating decisions are typically not taught in an academic setting. In addition, over a 40-year career, I have rarely seen a focus on value-creating decision making in a workplace setting. Yet, employees are expected to make value-creating decisions quickly and effectively. Most employees lack the information or training on how to do this. As we progress in our careers, more accountability is granted to us. Typically, the greater the levels of accountability, the more value-creating decisions are expected. Experience does not always dictate whether decision making will improve (I have seen more than a few bad decisions made at very senior levels).

A good defensive strategy for any company in the current, fast-paced, sometimes unpredictable business environment, is the ability to make good decisions. Making value-creating decisions helps ensure that the company remains profitable and strategically competitive. Companies rank effective decision making high on the list of desirable traits when recruiting new employees. These are just some of the reasons why it benefits each of us to learn more about how to be a good decision maker.

Book Overview for Project Decision Making

This book is not intended to be a comprehensive instruction manual for supply chain professionals. There are plenty of great books on the market that already satisfy that need. It is also not a book focused on the fundamentals of project management; again, there are lots of books that can guide project managers. Instead, the book takes a different, multidisciplinary approach (project management, supply chain, risk, operations, and strategy) and uses a framework to provide parameters for supply chain project decision making.

The goal is to teach the fundamentals of making a value-creating supply chain project decision; decisions that efficiently expend a minimal number of resources create opportunities, revenue, and ultimately profit for a company. This will be introduced formally in the next chapter. The approach is to instill in readers an understanding of what a value-creating decision is and apply this to project management fundamental material and theory. Readers then combine this with their own unique knowledge and experience of their particular industry to make better supply chain project decisions.

To help understand the approach, I provide a personal example. Years ago, I was working for a major gasoline retailer and refiner. One of my roles was to turn operations around for a region which included a team of hundreds of employees at multiple retail sites. One of our brand offerings included small kiosks where our company was partnered with a major retailer. In addition to the gasoline product offering, we also sold a minimal number of cigarettes (low margin), lottery tickets (very low margin), and some confectionary.

One day, I was having a conversation with one of my area managers. The manager told me that she was really trying to promote the kiosk sales. It dawned on me that she had no idea how we made money, or rather, made a profit at the branded kiosks. I was gob struck. I had assumed that all my direct reports knew about the fundamentals of this industry and were using these to make value-creating decisions. It was also clear that this area manager did not understand what drove the profit (and loss) within the financial statements. Without these fundamentals, it was impossible for this area manager (leading multiple sites and hundreds of employees) to make value-creating decisions. She did not have the right decision making data and criteria and did not understand the fundamentals of this industry and how our company competed to win. Therefore, she was making rudimentary decisions (Figure 1.1).

My comment to her was: "If you can find where we are 1 cent lower in gasoline pricing than our competitors in the market and if we move the price up, we will make more profit from that one penny than your kiosk will make in the whole year." We worked through the numbers and she was amazed.

Very quickly, this astute area manager was sharing what she had learned with her store managers. Then, about a week later, something amazing happened; I started getting phone calls from her store managers

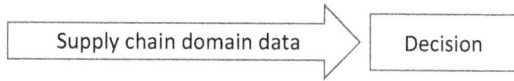

Figure 1.1 Rudimentary decision making

to discuss gas prices and why we had not raised the price by a penny or two. When people understand why they do what they do and what their role is in creating value, they often change the effort they exert in their job. Furthermore, once people understand the fundamentals of what drives value in their own industry, they can align this with their role in the company to make value-creating project decisions.

Over my career, I have recognized that when people in the workplace understand why they are doing something, they behave differently and make different decisions. Often, people are never told why but rather just told to do something. So, we do it the best we can but usually with half a heart. Besides, we all have too much to do in our workplace to give everything 110 percent. So, choices are made. We believe we are focused on the right activities and doing good work. However, unless we understand our industry fundamentals, along with the theory outlined in this book, we may, in fact, be wasting valuable company resources as the area manager was doing.

A final note on value-creating decisions. Although the bulk of this book examines making value-creating project decisions for profit-making companies, those decisions extend into all streams of our community including nonprofit companies. Nonprofit companies focus on how to deliver a product or service to the customers and communities they serve. They, like all companies, have limited resources. Therefore, it is in a nonprofit company's best interest to know the same supply chain fundamentals in order to expend the least number of resources while serving their customers.

Part I—Supply Chain Project Decision Fundamentals

The first part of this book focuses on the foundational material required to make value-creating project decisions. Knowledge about decision making, project management, risk, and strategy helps us to understand what value-creating decisions entail. Note that this book will not dive into the full discipline of supply chain, such as warehousing, distribution, off-shoring, or other important supply chain key topics. There are many other books out there that can provide this information. The purpose of this book is to provide the fundamentals of supply chain decision making in order to make value-creating project decisions. Once the fundamentals are understood, they can be applied to those other topics, such as warehousing.

Integrating domain data with project management data including concepts, tools, and processes will improve the quality of decisions along with how to implement them (Figure 1.2).

Chapter 2 introduces the reader to value-creating decisions. These decisions are executed in the form or projects. Therefore, the fundamentals of project management are also introduced in this chapter. Both of these concepts form the core of this book and are woven into each chapter.

Chapter 3 focuses on the topic of decision making. Consider the following quote: A decision is an irrevocable allocation of resources.[4] Every single time a decision is made, resource utilization has begun. This means that company resources, including money, people, and time, cannot come back once used. Therefore, understanding the importance of decision making, along with decision making processes, forms a key part of making value-creating decisions.

Chapter 4 ties decisions into decision making criteria, including company strategy and goals. The criteria must be considered and included in all supply chain project decisions. This step builds on simply applying domain data and instead helps ensure decisions are aligned with the corporate identity and direction (Figure 1.3).

Chapter 5 discusses the importance of risk and decision making. Risk is present in everything we do. Value-creating decisions must be aligned to a company's tolerance for risk. What is considered risky to

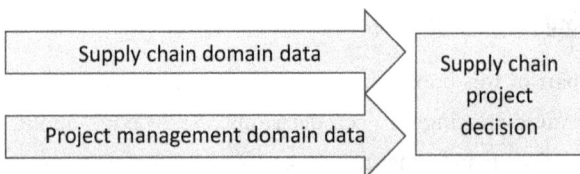

Figure 1.2 Supply chain and project management decisions

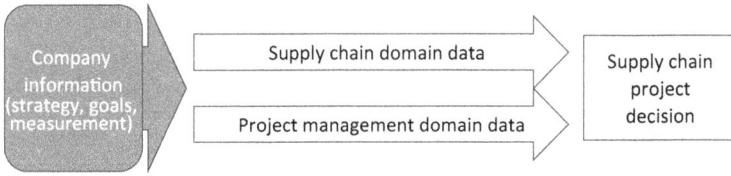

Figure 1.3 Alignment of decision making data and criteria

one person or a company may not be considered risky to another person or company. This step is intended to further increase the probability of generating value-creating project decisions (Figure 1.4).

Part II—Application of Supply Chain Project Decisions

The second part of this book focuses on the application of the material to two specific types of supply chain opportunities: services and make-or-buy decisions. These are both considered unique in their decision making needs and can be difficult to do well.

Chapter 6 shifts into the application of the material starting with make-or-buy project decisions. These decisions examine whether a company should produce a good or service internally (intra-company) or outsource that activity to an external supplier. The chapter includes the theoretical and foundational decision making criteria so that readers can apply their make-or-buy decisions to off-shore, near-shore, or other outsourcing possibilities.

Chapter 7 provides information and theory for making service supply chain project decisions. Service supply chains were included in this book because the focus on supply chain management is often only on the movement of physical goods. These are far easier to measure and discuss. Services can be abstract and more difficult to quantify

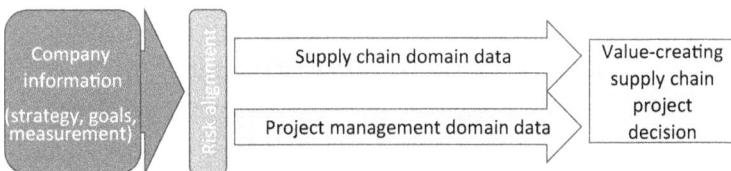

Figure 1.4 Alignment of decision making criteria to reduce project risk

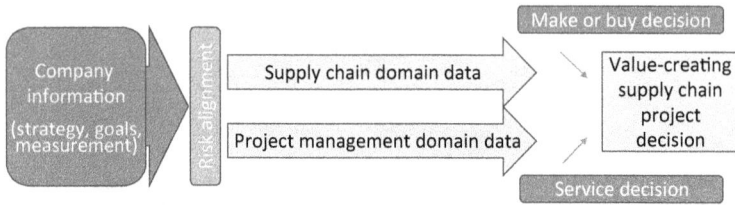

Figure 1.5 Incorporating decision making fundamentals for value-creating supply chain project decisions

to make good value-creating decisions. For example, how are project decisions made to procure a service such as a consultant, an engineer, or an electrician; how will their work be evaluated and measured? This is a very important topic because services make up the majority of everything a country produces in most industrialized countries, and yet, most people say these decisions are the most difficult to make. There is value in understanding how service supply chain project decisions differ from physical goods.

In summary, Part I provides the foundation for good decision making and Part II applies the material to specific types of supply chain project decisions (Figure 1.5).

Finally, Chapter 8 includes what every good project should have: a lessons learned section. It also includes a short section on material relevant to making value-creating supply chain decisions but which was excluded from this book and why it was excluded.

Application Questions

1. Discuss the role of supply chain professionals in business today.
2. Some examples were provided in this chapter regarding how our supply chains have evolved and provide examples from your experience.
3. Regardless of what position you hold, discuss how your role contributes to creating a value in your company.
4. Discuss why the area manager, in my example, is not alone in that many people are unable to make value-creating decisions.

CHAPTER 2

Fundamentals for Project Decision Making

Learning Objectives

- Discuss the importance of a framework for decision making and how a framework can be leveraged to make a value-creating decision.
- Explain Porter's Value Chain framework.
- Learn about project management fundamentals and how these can be applied for making value-creating decisions.

The first section introduces the concept of value-creating decisions. To understand how value is created in a company, Porter's value chain framework is laid out. Frameworks are useful tools for communicating core concepts of a subject matter in a visual format.

The subsequent section introduces project management fundamentals. Projects embody a company's strategy. Therefore, there is an essential link between value-creating decisions and how these are executed in the form of projects. Both of these concepts form the core of this book and are woven into each subsequent chapter.

A Framework for Making Value-Creating Project Decisions

The purpose of a company strategy is to lay out how a company competes and creates value in the industry it operates within. Over time, each company searches for new ways to add value; this is updated in their competitive strategy. All projects must reflect how they will support the achievement of the strategy. Strategy sets the overarching direction for the entire company and therefore provides direction for all employees.

In addition, every function in the company must have its own strategy (aligned with the corporate strategy), goals, and unique processes for getting its work done. The supply chain strategy should outline how the company will source and procure its products and services.

In Chapter 4—Strategy, Goals, and Measurement—I discuss how to align project decisions with the goals and strategy. This section provides an overview of a business framework used throughout this book. It is used to define how goods and services flow into, through, and out of the company and demonstrates how it delivers their products or services. Second, it serves as a roadmap on how to plan and implement company strategy. Third, it is a tool used to guide and govern employee decision making by providing "guardrails" or parameters for making decisions. Fourth, when we know how a company creates value, all project decisions should focus on means to increase (or replace) value.

To achieve the corporate strategy, there must be alignment across functions in how work is to be performed. For example, consider how many functions at Amazon are involved in a single customer order—the order desk, movement of products from thousands of suppliers across the globe, shipping companies, accounts receivable, and multiple warehouses, to name a few. To move these products effectively and efficiently, there must be coordination across activities and geography. Outputs from one function will become the inputs for another.

Companies are living systems made up of numerous sub systems called functions, which interact in order to produce a good or service. These include functional titles such as marketing, operations, human resources, accounting, and information technology. Each function requires inputs (e.g., raw materials) and transforms them in some way to produce an output (e.g., a good or service). The output from one function is often an input to another function. For example, at a bakery, the baker will use flour and eggs as inputs to make and bake a cake. The finished product for the baker is a cake. The cake is an input for the cake decorator, along with the decorator's icing and tools. Further, all functions require resources (i.e., employees, cash, materials [icing], and so on) in order to complete their transformation process. Projects can impact the flow of how these functions work together to create a value.

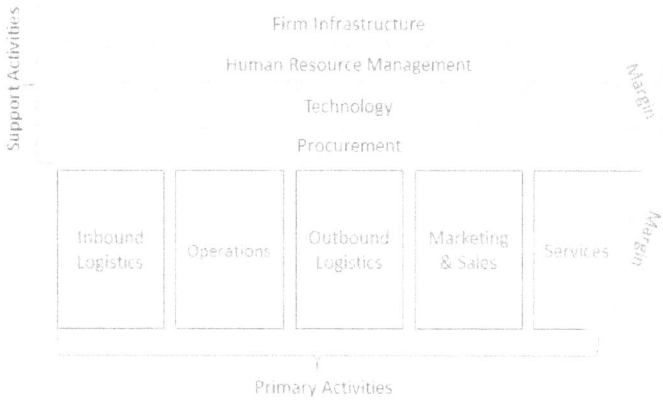

Figure 2.1 Value chain

Source: Citation 1—Michael Porter.

Incorporating Porter's value chain as a framework enables us to see the big picture while demonstrating how activities within a company are linked together (Figure 2.1). It provides a framework for how value-creating decisions can be made.

The value chain focuses on a company's activities (by the functions) required to produce a good or service and, ultimately, create value for its customers. A "value chain" is defined as "the set of discrete activities that must be accomplished to design, build, sell and distribute a product or service."[2] The framework visually lays out the company functions involved in that endeavor.[1] It includes the primary activities directly involved in creating goods and services. This is where the company value is created. It also includes the support activities that are indirectly involved and supports the primary activities.

There are five primary activities occurring in a sequence. First: inbound logistics, which are the inputs required to produce the goods and services. This includes the raw materials along with the warehouses to store them. Second: operations, which convert the inputs into an output (a good or service). Third: outbound logistics move and hold the finished goods. They also include the information flow from operations to the end-user. Fourth: marketing and sales that help communicate and create a market for and a demand for the product and service. Last: after-sales service and support for customers.

Next are the support activities. Their purpose is to enable the primary activities. For example, for a retail chain to operate effectively, human resources provide employee benefit programs to attract and retain qualified individuals to the company. The technology team provides the hardware and software required to support business operations. They might also enable access to data required for decision making. Firm infrastructure includes functions such as finance and accounting, which produce financial reports. The support activities are not directly involved in the production of goods and services but hold a critical support role in that they can make primary activities more effective.

What is the relationship between a supply chain and Porter's value chain? Because a supply chain includes all the resources and processes required to produce and sell a product or service from raw materials to the customer, the value chain graphically lays out where the value is created within a company. It is woven through the primary activities of the company's value chain and connects them to the entire value system (e.g., suppliers and their value chains). The system outlines how a company works collaboratively outside their borders with suppliers, distributors, and customers to create a competitive advantage.

The importance of supply chain management is closely tied to the benefits it creates for the company along with other companies linked within the supply chain.[3] The efficiency and effectiveness by which these are connected will determine the costs and, ultimately, the profit of the company. Project concepts must support the flow across the chain and demonstrate how they can add value.

Note that all five primary activities are required to create value. Exactly how the value chain activities are executed will determine the costs and the ability of the company to generate a profit. In addition, a competitive advantage (above-average profitability) is created through primary activities.

Business processes are the means for achieving work in a company. They link both primary and support activities. For example, a process might focus on the steps at a restaurant to take a customer's order, how an employee can order office supplies, or how to pay a supplier.

A well-functioning system will have clear and efficient processes and ensure continuity across the company. They help define how the functions should effectively work together. Projects have their own unique processes; these are laid out later in the chapter.

Both project and business processes help determine whether and how much value is created. When processes are too rigorous or cumbersome, or when they miss steps, timely production of goods and services becomes difficult due to wasted resources, duplication of effort, and unclear roles and responsibilities.

Every company interacts with their stakeholders, which include customers, suppliers, and regulators. In addition, external stakeholders provide feedback to the company. For example, whether customers are satisfied with the products and services of the company or if there are any regulatory changes. Porter captures this in a value chain system, which includes the company, suppliers providing inputs (and their value chains), and distributors shipping finished products to customers. It is woven through the primary activities of the company's value chain and connects them to the entire value system (e.g., suppliers and their value chains). The system outlines how a company works collaboratively outside their borders with suppliers, distributors, and customers to create a competitive advantage. Collaborating with key stakeholders can provide timely information about the value chain system and help to prevent supply chain disruptions or recognize market opportunities.

So far, we have discussed a framework used to outline how the activities produce goods and services and the functions that do the work, and how the functions can effectively work together to produce goods and services and create value. When a company takes action to implement company strategy (corporate or functional), it shifts from its day-to-day operations into project mode. Because a project is a temporary endeavor, it requires different processes than those of day-to-day operational decision making. Therefore, strategic decisions embodied in a project require their own unique governance and processes.

Porter's value chain is used to provide the framework outlining the primary and support activities. However, achieving a project goal may include redefining the relationships, processes, and governance that already exist. An introduction to project management is reviewed next. This material will be applied to making value-creating decisions.

Project Management Fundamentals

When we consider projects, we might think about constructing a new bridge or renovating a house. However, projects take many different forms for different purposes. Companies may have hundreds of projects underway at any point in time. Methods to improve operations and increase productivity, empowered and demanding consumers, complexity of supply chains, regulatory challenges, and advances in technology[4] are all reasons for a company to revisit the company and supply chain strategy. A project embodies the needed changes and is the vehicle to achieve the strategy. Incorporating project management theory and processes will be used to make value-creating supply chain decisions.

A project is defined as "... A temporary endeavor undertaken to create a unique product, service or result."[5] A project is temporary, which means that at some point the project will either be completed and "operationalized" or deemed to no longer be needed or feasible, and the project team disbands. There is no defined time period for a project; it could take days or years. Most supply chain project decisions can take a few months; however, larger, more strategic projects, such as a large acquisition, can take longer, even years. Each project is unique. For example, building a warehouse in one city will not be like building one in another city, as issues such as permits, suppliers, regulatory laws and bylaws, and available materials may all be different.

Projects vary from the ongoing operations of a company. Ongoing operations have defined and repeated processes for getting work done. For example, the accounts payable function uses the same process using the same technology, has defined people doing the work, and produces the same report each week for the same employees. A project steps out of the day-to-day operations and, therefore, requires unique project processes. For example, should the payable function determine that the existing technology will not meet a regulatory change, a project should be launched to determine how to resolve the issue. Perhaps a request for proposal (RFP) could be issued to source a new technology supplier.

Projects and ongoing operations are similar in that the operations or the project are both performed by people, each is constrained by limited resources, and there is a period of planning followed by executing the work, which includes a control process overseeing how the work is completed.[5] The major difference between the two is that operations are ongoing and repetitive while each project is unique and temporary.[5]

Project management is defined as "...the application of knowledge, skills, tools and techniques to project activities to meet project requirements."[5] Projects exist to satisfy a business need that cannot be accomplished in the day-to-day operations. They can be initiated by any function and by any level of employee, but usually require support from a senior leader. In addition, every project must demonstrate how it will achieve a company's goal(s) in support of the corporate strategy and, ultimately, show how it will create increased value. Because of this, most projects are initiated by the function carrying out the "primary activities" as they are the revenue-generating arm of the company. For example, supply chain projects may focus on how resources are sourced and distributed along with the processes associated with resource movement. This is the statement of work (SOW) which outlines what you plan to deliver and includes how the project goals will align with the company goals.

Each project is divided into sequential phases and ends with the project becoming operationalized (or abandoned if not feasible). These phases collectively make up the life cycle of the project.[6] While the title given to each phase varies slightly from company to company (note: some companies, especially smaller companies, may have no project management governance, tools, or processes), in general, a project is initiated to achieve a strategy and exists in this phase as a concept. During the next phase, the concept is further defined and built out. During this phase, feasibility, along with exactly how the project will create new value for the company, is determined. This includes shifting from a mere concept to very detailed design and drawings, including a complete financial and risk analysis.

Next, the project is implemented. For example, if the project is a new warehouse, this is the stage where it moves from paper drawings to a physical structure. At this point, the project will impact the primary activities as to how the work is being done currently and how it will be done in the future. The changes can be minimal, with limited impact to a single function (or sub function), or they can drastically change how the company creates value, which can necessitate significant resources, time, and leadership support.

During the final phase, the project planning and execution are completed, and the product or service is delivered to the client. The project will be officially closed as it has become operationalized. Analyzing the lessons learned is an important activity for this phase. This includes project team members discussing and documenting what worked well and where there were issues on the project. It should also include how the team arrived at some of their decisions and any recommendations for future similar projects.

The Project Management Institute (PMI) includes five process groups which can be repeated within each phase of the project. The first process group is termed "initiating," which defines a new project or new phase of an existing project.[6] The second phase is "planning," where progressively more detail is planned out for the project. This includes delimiting the scope, refining the objectives, and defining the course of action required[6]. Third is "executing," which integrates people and other resources required to execute the project plan. "Monitoring and controlling" ensure that the work outlined in the plan is occurring and to the level of quality required to meet the project objectives. Last, "closing" process is where the project, phase, or contract is completed.[6]

Stakeholders are a key component of any project. There are different classifications of stakeholders, each requiring varying levels of consideration and communication. First are the key, or primary, stakeholders. The title typically given to the leader of the primary stakeholders is the "project sponsor." The sponsor provides clarity on the reason for the project and how it will achieve the goals of the corporate strategy. While the sponsorship role may vary slightly depending on the project, usually a senior leader provides the necessary resources and has the accountability for delivering a successful project. There are additional primary stakeholders who will be directly impacted by the project. In general, these are the employees who reside within the sponsor's span of control. These stakeholders will help to define the project objectives, provide valuable input, and will be the recipients of the completed project product or service. Secondary stakeholders also have a vested interest in the project and may encounter changes in how they complete their work after the project is operationalized. For example, while their core job does not change, a weekly report for the secondary stakeholders may come in a different format and on a different day. These changes require a level of consultation and communication.

In addition to primary and secondary stakeholders, there are additional stakeholders who can include any or all employees in a company who seek to know relevant information about changes associated with the project. This group can also include the community in which the company operates. Identifying who can be impacted by a project and who might have a vested interest is an important study to undertake. For example, stakeholders can include other members of the value system, such as suppliers and customers, and be classified as primary, secondary, or other interested parties. Failing to identify an important group can impact the success of a project. Many projects have received bad publicity or been derailed because of the failure to consult with all relevant stakeholders in the community a company operates within.

Managing stakeholders has become an important part of any project. Awareness of how a project might impact stakeholders, both internal to the company and external, is required so that a communication and change plan can be developed to prepare and support stakeholders in adapting to the changes associated with the project. Change management is a discipline that helps to build awareness of upcoming changes. A comprehensive, strategic change plan can be developed, which outlines how to enable the different stakeholder groups to understand, provide input into, and, in the end, adapt to the change. Including an experienced and qualified change person in high-impact projects will help the project achieve the goals in the most efficient and effective manner.

Because projects exist outside of the day-to-day operations, the business processes associated with executing work in the value chain are not designed to govern how work is completed in a project. The PMI has developed 44 project management processes, used to govern the work within a project. These processes are grouped into nine knowledge areas that provide guidance and governance for the practices, inputs, outputs, tools, and techniques associated with a project.[5] Next, we will discuss each of the nine knowledge areas and how each of these areas relates to making value-creating decisions.

1. Project Integration Management

The work required to complete a project requires resource coordination. In addition, the project interfaces with the company to interact with the primary stakeholders. The project team may also need to interact with stakeholders who are external to the company, such as suppliers, customers, or the community the company operates within. This is necessary in order to access and coordinate resources required for the project. Project integration across the project phases is required for resource continuity. Therefore, integration processes focus on the activities required to identify, define, combine, unify, and coordinate the scope of work identified for the project.[5] A well-thought-out integration plan uses the right company resources at the right time and causes minimal disruption to the primary activities to complete the project in an efficient manner.

Integration also includes working with the primary stakeholders as they will be impacted by the supply chain project. They may have changes to their jobs, the technology they use, and the processes they use to complete their work. In order to be ready to accept the change associated with the project, an integration plan needs to be developed and is called a "business readiness plan."

2. Project Scope Management

The scope processes identify the work required to complete the project and achieve the goals (purpose) of the project. The scope plan should also note what is not included in the project, so that stakeholders are clear on what is in and out of scope. Clarity on the strategy and goal of the project will help define the scope.

A critical component of scope management is developing a work breakdown structure (WBS). It is a hierarchical diagram starting with a high-level overview of the project and moving progressively toward more detail in each subsequent lower level. Most WBS diagrams often have four levels in the structure. The lowest level of a WBS contains the most detail and should be granular enough to enable a high-quality estimate, which can be assigned to a supplier, group, or contractor to complete. Each of these is termed a "work package." The WBS is an important tool where resources can be assigned (e.g., an electrician) to each work package along with the estimated time (refer to #3 Time) to complete the work and a cost estimate (refer to #4 Cost, and #9 Procurement). Note: these references to the other knowledge areas should also serve to demonstrate the importance of #1—Integration.

Constructing a WBS starts early in the project and becomes more granular through the detailed planning process. Collectively, all the work packages will deliver the finished project. For example, designing and constructing a new warehouse might be the project. There may be hundreds of work packages ranging from sourcing land and obtaining building permits to pouring concrete, as well as providing electrical and other trades required to complete the project. A well-designed WBS will minimize the resources required and help keep the project on time and budget in order to achieve the strategic goal.

3. Project Time Management

The processes in this knowledge area focus on completing the project in a timely manner. Using the WBS, the project manager will estimate the time to complete each work package and arrange the work packages into a sequenced schedule. The schedule can be viewed with primary (and secondary) stakeholders along with the contractors and others completing the work. This ensures that all stakeholders are aware of what changes are forthcoming and when they will be impacted.

4. Project Cost Management

This knowledge area focuses on "the processes involved in planning, estimating, budgeting, and controlling costs so that the project can be completed within the approved budget."[7] The WBS is required to complete the estimating process. The lowest level of the WBS includes all the work packages; each of these require an estimate (refer to #9 Procurement). Once each work package has been estimated, a final budget can be developed and presented to the project sponsor for final approval. A well-thought-out WBS is the starting point for achieving good cost estimates.

5. Project Quality Management

Quality is an abstract concept. The PMI defines "quality" as "the degree to which a set of inherent characteristics fulfills requirements."[8] In general, quality is associated with price and longevity. A simple example: there is a difference in quality between buying 1-day-old roses and 1-week-old roses (wilting, dropping petals, turning brown and so on)— the quality varies significantly as should the price. Quality processes include quality planning, performing quality assurance, and performing quality control.[5]

There are a few qualifiers with quality. First, the work included in the WBS adheres to any company policies, objectives, and responsibilities required by the project. Second, the company receives what was outlined in the work package; this is called "quality control." Receiving less quality than required can impact safety, company reputation, returns, and recalls, and there are many other tangible and intangible issues. Value-creating decisions ensure that the quality required adheres to company policies, and regulatory and safety requirements, in order to protect people and the community and maintain company's reputation.

6. Project Human Resource Management

This involves managing the people who are assigned to roles and responsibilities for the successful completion of the project. There is usually a project management team that includes the project manager and any other key people (employees, contractors, and others) on the project. The team usually stays intact throughout the project. Some projects might be smaller in scope and may only require a project manager.

Aside from the project team, other people involved in the project may ebb and flow throughout the project. First, the employees or the contractors who will complete each work package and may come and go on the project as per the schedule. Second, the project team will interface and integrate with primary stakeholders to establish and ensure business readiness for the successful completion of the project. Having the right people on the project at the right time ensures the right level and type of decision making and expertise.

7. Project Communications Management

Project communications includes a variety of activities, all required for the successful completion of the project. First, stakeholder communication requires interacting with both primary and secondary stakeholders and others to provide information, updates, and, at times, feedback on the project progress. Stakeholders often span a wide variety of people from key stakeholders, who have a vested interest in the project's success, from the CEO to secondary stakeholders, such as company employees who appreciate a monthly update newsletter. Second, performance reporting provides a formal update, including progress measurement and forecasting. Each stakeholder group should have a needs assessment so that relevant information can be supplied to each group in a timely manner.

8. Project Risk Management

PMI defines a risk as "an uncertain event or condition that, if it occurs, has a positive or negative effect on one or more project objectives."[9] Risk management includes "the processes concerned with conducting risk management planning, identification, analysis, responses, and monitoring and control on a project."[10] Risks can occur within the project and team, the company, or external to the company, such as with a supplier or a regulatory change. Because of this, risk management begins early in the project and continues throughout. A person's experience with a risk topic and how they view the "riskiness" of something will impact what decision they take. Based on this, all of Chapter 5, has been devoted to the topic of risk.

9. Project Procurement Management

To procure is to acquire something. Procurement is a process of sourcing, acquiring, and paying for goods and services. As defined earlier, supply chain management coordinates the functions for the purposes of improving the long-term performance of the individual companies and the supply chain. It includes all the resources and processes required to produce and sell a product or service from raw materials to the customer. It is woven through the primary activities of the company's value chain and connects these to the entire value system. Therefore, decisions on which goods and services to procure will impact the efficiency and effectiveness of operations.

Given the significant impact, cost, and time in procuring products and services, many large companies devote full-time resources to this activity in the procurement function. Projects are no exception. The project goal(s) must align with company strategy and statement of work. Therefore, the procurement decisions on the project must carefully evaluate and ensure that any changes made to existing resource acquisition will achieve project goals and are consistent with risk management policies.

Procurement includes sourcing suppliers that meet company requirements and project goals, particularly in terms of quality. It also includes all aspects of administering contracts or purchase orders along with administering ongoing contracts with suppliers.

Procuring a service requires special attention. Make-or-buy decisions do too. Both are important topics and, therefore, are each covered in their own chapter.

This section provides a very quick overview of project management along with some key tools and processes to use when making supply chain decisions. Omitted were some important details such as a document called a "project charter" (defined as: "a document issued by the project initiator or sponsor that formally authorizes the existence of a project.").[11] You should know your own company's formal processes to ensure you are aligned with the requirements and governance. Alternatively, seek out the many excellent resources offered by the PMI.

In summary, supply chain decisions are considered project decisions. Project decisions fall outside of the regular day-to-day operational decisions and will shift how work is done in the value chain. Therefore, these decisions require unique processes and parameters provided by project management tools and the nine project management knowledge areas.

Summary

This chapter provided two key fundamental topics required for value-creating project decisions. First, Porter's value chain. Frameworks are important communication tools to convey meaningful concepts in a domain. Because a company operates as a system, all parts must work effectively together to create value. The value chain lays out where the value is created in a company and how the system must work together to create value.

Next, fundamental project management theory and tools. Strategy is the means for creating new or additional value. Projects embody strategy. Therefore, a project must be aligned with the strategy the company intends to achieve. To create value in the form or a project, project management tools were introduced. This foundational theory is applied and built upon in subsequent chapters.

Application Questions

1. Explain the link between business processes and Porter's value chain.

2. Discuss how project management tools and processes can be used to create value in a company.

3. Discuss how Porter's value chain can help support value-creating supply chain project decisions.

CHAPTER 3

Decision Making for Projects

Learning Objectives

- Determine how good decisions lead to good business project results.
- Discuss how rational decisions differ from intuitive decisions.
- Identify the process to becoming a good decision maker who can make value-creating project decisions.
- Discuss the role technology has with decision making and how technology is disrupting decision making in the workplace.

Importance of Project Decision Making

The mere fact that you are reading this book suggests that you made a decision. Decisions are an important part of our everyday life; in fact, the average person makes about 35,000 decisions each day. If we subtract the time we are sleeping (and not consciously aware of decisions we may be making), then a decision is made approximately every 2 seconds. Some of these 35,000 decisions are made quickly and without much thought, such as when to take another sip of our coffee or cross our legs at our desk.

Most of the 35,000 decisions a person makes every day are done subconsciously. Of the conscious and purposeful decisions we make, many are made each day in our jobs. Often these types of decisions require problem solving and critical thinking. Many employers rate these types of decisions as essential skills when recruiting new employees. There has been a significant increase in the number of jobs that require these skills, including management-level jobs. In fact, the availability of these jobs has more than doubled from 15 to 32 percent over the last 50 years.[1]

The increase is even more pronounced in high-growth industries and the private sector.

Conversely, researchers have found that in all sectors of the economy, there are an increasing number of simple and routine tasks which can now be managed by technology and require no human involvement. Large volumes of data can easily be programed to provide valuable insights and make predictions, replacing the need for basic, simple decisions. For example, using an online chat with a large retailer is often done with a simple algorithmic formula where common and predictable questions can be answered by a machine, for example, regarding operating hours or store locations. This action is performed by a "bot," an automated system that has been programed to do certain tasks.

Algorithmic formulas are getting better at predicting and resolving simple, high predictability, low variance, and one-dimensional problems. Companies are beginning to replace these types of jobs (or aspects of the job) with computers as they can do the job with accuracy. These systems are becoming so good that they can provide customers with account information (once the computer has verified the customer) and troubleshoot problems.

Once a customer has maneuvered through this bot-managed system and still has questions, the bot can move the customer to a live, knowledgeable customer service representative who can actively engage with the customer. This process frees up the need to have many customer service representatives and instead retains those who can provide more value-creating information for their customers. An experienced customer service representative will engage directly with the customer to resolve their questions. This interaction requires judgment and experience by the customer service representative.

The value for employers resides with focusing their experienced employee representatives on value-creating work, such as generating project concepts that create value for the company. For employees, this helps with job satisfaction. This also helps customers who receive products and services that fulfill needs.

Because of the importance of decision making, it behooves us to define and understand what a decision is, how decisions are made, when and why they are made, and how we can get better at making decisions. Learning what it takes to become a more capable decision maker is the focus of this chapter. Subsequent chapters build on this foundation and provide relevant supply chain decision making criteria. A good foundation is intended to help advance our careers and build stronger relationships both in and out of the workplace.

Defining the Term "Decision"

To make a value-creating decision, let us start by defining what a "decision" is. There are many definitions; a few of these will be discussed and analyzed. First, a simple definition: "The act of making up one's mind."[2] This suggests that choices are conscious and eliminate the simple, unconscious, and automatic decisions made each day. A second definition states that: "Decisions are choices over a set of potential actions."[3] Similar to the first, but this suggests that there are options associated with a decision, and that we may not be restricted or bound by one choice. However, this implies that there is some work or thinking to be done before arriving at a decision.

Let us consider that the concept of decision making conveys it as being a conscious act, and the next definition provides further insight into defining what is a decision:

> A decision is a deliberate choice of a course of action that is made after a consideration of alternative choices, with a view toward reaching a certain desired outcome. The deliberateness distinguishes it from an impulse, whim, or reflex, although many people do not heed this distinction. The outcome sought is usually the solution of a problem, the meeting of a need, or the realizing of an opportunity.[4]

This definition builds on the previous two and provides a foundation for supply chain decisions. First, it definitively separates out subconscious decisions and focuses on those which seem to be more important. Second, it includes key words such as "consideration" and "choice." A choice suggests that there is criteria associated with the opportunity so that an ideal decision can be made. The criteria built within this definition is a "desired outcome," "meeting of a need," and "realization of an opportunity." Project decisions begin with understanding the company's strategy and goals and must be aligned with them. Last, there must be an understanding of how the company operates and competes within its industry and how it recognizes opportunities and then makes decisions. These three reasons provide a foundation for making supply chain decisions and distinguish decisions from being strictly impulsive.

The fourth and final definition builds on the other three and makes an impactful statement: "an irrevocable allocation of resources."[5] Short and to the point while packing in so much meaning. First, there are resources associated with projects. Resources include suppliers, customers, employees, time, money, and assets, to name a few. Resource usage requires a commitment from the resource owner in order to obtain that usage (i.e., use, borrow, or have access), such as a project charter approved by the project sponsor.

Second, it is the responsibility of the project manager to determine which resources are required for making a supply chain project decision. By applying the relevant knowledge areas, a project manager can determine which resources are required. For example, a work breakdown structure is a good starting point. Third, there is a cost to using resources—people have limited time and will already be committed to other work (the ability to multi task is limited in success!). Therefore, a decision involves careful thought and consideration, given the cost of resources required.

Finally, decisions require understanding the impact on the primary activities associated with Porter's value chain and can impact resources associated with the whole company. Decisions made in isolation (those that benefit only the function or sub function) might have a negative impact on the company. For example, a decision to discontinue an annual supplier lunch can save money, but it may have hidden costs such as lost networking opportunities or learning more about the products and services the supplier is planning. Or for example, suppose one project suggestion was accepted over other competing projects. This may leave idle resources which could have been used more productively and produced more for the company than the selected project. Decision makers may have to answer for the results of their decision. Therefore, this final definition of a decision suggests a decision can impact the resources, profitability, and reputation of a company.

So far, we have defined what a decision is, and the importance of good decision making. But exactly how do we become better decision makers and develop this critical skill? Decision making models are explored next, followed by a section on how we can improve our decision making ability. Understanding and managing risk also plays a critical role in helping us become better decision makers. This concept is explored more in Chapter 5—Risk.

Decision Making Models

Different types of decisions require different approaches to making a decision. Two of the more well-used models are discussed next.

Rational Decisions

"Rational," by definition, means using reason or logic. The first step in making a rational decision is to acknowledge that a decision needs to be made. Relevant information associated with the decision needs to be included. For example, acknowledging a decision needs to be made to ship a package from city A to city B. Relevant information likely includes the receiver's name, the size and weight of the package, as well as important criteria such as whether the package contains a perishable good, for example, an organ for organ transplant surgery and, therefore, requires rush delivery. In general, company processes, such as project processes, follow a rational approach.

The next step in making a rational decision is generating alternatives. To transport packages, options might include trucks, trains, or airplanes, among others. The third step is to assess the options associated with the decision; for example, how much time is required to transport and arrive at the destination, what is the supplier's geographical coverage, or their reputation. This step requires that adequate information be gathered so that a rational decision can be made. Often a decision made in our jobs is based upon cost; however, having relevant and pertinent criteria (e.g., whether a perishable product is involved) will expand the complexity of the decision and require more consideration. Once the options have been assessed and evaluated, an option is selected, and the decision maker moves toward implementation. For example, two transportation companies are evaluated to ensure they each meet the criteria required for transportation of the perishable product.

The last step in making a rational choice is evaluating the result of the decision. This is important to know if a good decision was made based upon the available information at the time. To be able to evaluate whether the decision was successful, there must be feedback. For example, if a package was delivered per the contract along with other relevant information, such as damage to the package. This information will help determine whether our rational decision proved correct and, therefore, beneficial.

A rational decision making model is widely used in business for a variety of reasons. First, a rational decision follows a clear and orderly path from beginning to end. Shipping a package can be documented in a company process so that all employees involved in shipping a package can follow the same simple steps. Second, a rational decision making approach is intended to be objective and to use facts. In the shipping example, the costs involved can be evaluated in view of the mode of transportation selected. The model assumes the decision maker will make an optimal choice that can be defended and supported with evidence. Next, the method is easy to follow because it includes a few simple steps that can be easily taught or replicated for subsequent decisions.

Shortfalls in using a rational decision making model are as follows: First, the approach assumes the decision maker has all the information required in which to make a decision. We typically don't. Often, we will never have all the information required to make a good decision. People are limited by the availability of information. In addition, people have multiple tasks to complete at any one time and, therefore, may not have enough time to spend on a task to make an optimal decision. Therefore, the decision is made with the available time and resources on hand.

Second, a rational decision still requires judgment and experience to know when a person has "enough" information versus continuing to spend time and resources on making a decision. Third, humans are fallible and may not be aware of what information is important enough with which to make the decision, or where to look for information. Bias can sneak into our decision and cloud our judgment, such as a belief about a particular carrier or method of transportation. Finally, a rational decision "cleans the slate" each time. This means each time a rational decision is required, the exact same steps need to be followed. This suggests that we do not build experience or knowledge into the decision making process.

> On an important decision one rarely has 100 percent of the information needed for a good decision no matter how much one spends or how long one waits. And, if one waits too long, he has a different problem and has to start all over. This is the terrible dilemma of the hesitant decision maker.
>
> —Robert K. Greenleaf, The Servant as Leader

Intuitive Decisions

Intuitive decisions have been mistakenly labeled as "gut decisions." An intuitive decision is far more complex than just shooting from the gut or having a "gut feel." While an intuitive decision is not based on gut feel, it is also not a rational decision. The word "intuition" comes from the Latin word *in-tuir*, meaning "to know within."[6] These decisions are made so quickly because they are born of foundational experience that is based on similar situations. Our expertise comes from recognizing the current situation and comparing it to past similar situations. That experience builds a foundation that allows us to make fast decisions and not have to follow a rational decision making process each time a similar situation arises. Experience results from a variety of skills, ranging from years of doing a similar job or years of playing a sport or a musical instrument. Although each project concept is new and unique, research suggests that project decision making is based on intuition, which is years of experience based on similar situations.[9]

Learning Stages With Intuitive Decisions

There are five learning stages a person moves through in building experience and proficiency with a particular skill.[7] In order, from no or low experience to being proficient: novice, advanced beginner, competence, proficiency, and expert. We start as a "novice" where information is provided in a format in which the novice can make sense of the information without having the required skill. For example, a 16-year-old can attend a driver's education course held in a classroom and be able to understand information given by the instructor, yet the young person may have never previously driven a vehicle. The classroom experience provides foundational information for the 16-year-old to learn the skill of driving.

The second stage is the "advanced beginner" where a person gains experience by practicing the skill. Continuing with the learning-to-drive example, in this second stage the learner sits in the driver's seat and physically drives the vehicle (ideally the instructor is sitting beside the learner with their own steering wheel and brakes, supporting the learner as they practice the new skills!). Repeating the task builds useful experience. Practice and repetition help the learner move to the next stage, titled "competence," where the learner begins to determine what information in the domain is relevant to mastering the skill and then applies that information to making decisions. This could include identifiers such as speed signs, playground zones, or crosswalks that the new driver must carefully scout for. That information is taken in, processed, and becomes a basis for making good driving decisions. Likewise, information not relevant to the (driving) domain, and therefore not relevant to becoming a good driver, would include, for example, store signs or advertisements on the boulevard. This information should be screened out and ignored so that the driver remains attentive to information that is helpful to completing the skill of learning to drive.

Eventually, the driver becomes a competent driver with intuitive decisions beginning to replace reasoned responses. Thus, the learner is mastering the skill and no longer must watch for all the pieces of information with which to make a decision. They will come to know speed limits on residential streets and will get a feel for how much pressure to put on the pedal to keep a certain speed. They can contrast this with speed limits on a freeway or country highway. Experience will provide the driver with agood speed at which to merge onto the freeway. The speed at which the driver chooses to merge will be based on experience with decision making criteria, including traffic volume (low if late at night, or high if there are many vehicles in the morning commute) or road conditions, such as rain or construction on the highway. They will intuitively know which speed to select—no one needs to tell them. They do not have to follow a rational decision making process with questions such as "is it sunny or snowing" or "is it rush hour" or "is it late at night?" Further, merging onto the freeway should not be handled by a gut feeling! That's where accidents are certain to occur.

The fifth and final stage is becoming an "expert" at the skill. Experts can complete a task in any situation. When an expert receives domain information in a short period of time, based on their experience, they can quickly make an intuitive decision. Becoming an expert driver requires a wide variety of experiences. For example, a driver might easily adapt to situations such as driving in a large, populated city, on country roads with gravel, on the right or left side of the road, or in icy conditions. We have heard of heroic examples of expert airline pilots who have landed their airplane in almost any condition. These are intuitive decisions based on flying an aircraft for years in a wide variety of conditions.

At this stage, there is a big skill-level difference between the advanced beginner and the expert, or proficient person. For example, assume the advanced beginner is planning to drive on a freeway or highway for the first time. They may ask an experienced driver, "What speed should I be driving to successfully merge?" They will want an exact number because they lack experience merging at high speeds; they are not yet an intuitive driver. Contrast this with the experienced driver they are asking. An experienced driver will likely respond, "it depends." The experienced driver will consider weather conditions, such as rain or snow, or think about the time of day, considering issues such as rush hour versus nighttime.

There are numerous domain factors which contribute to making an intuitive response. Each of these factors aids the experienced driver form an intuitive response and merge appropriately. It will be an automatic and calm response. While their answer of "it depends" is accurate to any other experienced driver, this will likely frustrate the advanced beginner driver because they are looking for an exact speed so that they experience merging successfully. While this example may seem basic to most of us drivers, compare it to any question a new employee might ask in the workplace. To you, the answer might be obvious and even difficult to explain, but the new employee wants detailed information so that they do not make a mistake.

Moving from the beginner to one who is proficient at a skill takes time and practice. Recalling all the domain factors and steps is not easy for the proficient person because they have long forgotten the details that helped them to become proficient. A first-year university student might say their professor is very intelligent, but they also might state that their professor isn't a good teacher. Perhaps this is because the student is a novice or an advanced beginner in the subject matter and requires foundational information. The professor may have long forgotten the basic, foundational material in a domain that they themselves learned 10 or 20 years earlier, and now they are making intuitive decisions. Think back to the driving example and try to explain how to drive a car: "put the car in gear, keep your foot on the brake, look at your mirrors, give it a little bit of gas." Here is the first error— what is a "little bit of gas?" The instructor must explain this intuitive decision to the new driver, and it is not as easy as one might think. Of course, the inability to recall these steps can frustrate the person learning the new skill.

Perhaps one more point to help solidify intuitive decision making. Think about an experienced nurse assessing a patient. In time, a nurse no longer needs to refer to a checklist or read through school notes. Rest assured that they will follow a strict protocol; however, they will likely draw some basic conclusions on walking into a hospital room and visually assessing a patient. Or when a seasoned police officer pulls over a speeding car, the officer does not open an instruction manual or call more senior officers to ask for their opinion; training gave the officer this platform as a novice. The officer will follow strict procedures, but intuitive responses have long since replaced the need to open a manual for domain information and the need to follow a rational decision making process.

Domain knowledge for making intuitive decisions includes years of experience in whatever job(s) you work in. But intuitive decision making also includes the application of frameworks, theory, and concepts that we discuss in this chapter and throughout the book. Viewing a company through the lens of Porter's value chain framework, along with understanding more about decision making will support how value-creating supply chain decisions can be made. The next step is to learn more about the decision making process so that there is a foundation for how the tools and frameworks can be applied.

Data Inputs for Making a Decision

The process of good decision making has been noted as a required skill for employees in the current economy. Because of this, there has been a growing focus on understanding the process of decision making.[1] All decisions, rational, intuitive, projects, computer generated, or other, require data in order to make a decision.[1] For example, in shipping the package from point A to point B, the data required includes the supplier carriers, the information about the contents of our package and so on., There are three data-related inputs we need to make a decision.[1] The first is data quantity. How many carriers are enough, or how many become too much? Research notes that it is difficult to assess how much data are required and then which data to select in order to make a decision.

The second input is the amount of variance associated with the data. Obtaining different perspectives from a variety of people (i.e., data sources) provides a richer data set used to make a decision. This is why understanding stakeholders on a project is a critical data point. Often, there will either not be enough time or enough information to make the best decision, but a decision must be made. Last, and very important, is the data quality. Sources of data can be incomplete, old, biased, or have other problems.

Note that both humans and computers require the exact same data inputs in order to make a decision. The three were compared and contrasted between how a human versus a computer generates a decision.[1] First, data quantity. Computers can now take large amounts of data and very quickly generate algorithmic decisions that are useful for a company. Humans also use large amounts of data (experience) but also use judgment in determining which data to use to make a decision. introduce bias. This becomes more apparent with the other two components in the model.

The second input is variance with the data. With algorithmic decisions, it is difficult to accurately predict a solution. For humans, routine jobs with little variance suggests that we will learn our jobs and develop skills faster. However, over time, because our data quantity and variety do not change much, we become somewhat limited in our contribution and ability to move to more senior positions. Contrast this with a worker who is exposed to a higher variance of data early within their career. Recall the learning stages where a person moves through stages to build experience in a skill. However, people with high variances of data may take longer to build and master a domain of information, but eventually, more data produce a richer domain to draw from later in one's career. Unlike algorithmic decisions, today, humans can sift through variability in data better than a computer.

The final component in the model is data quality. Determining data quality begins with the raw data. A decision maker needs to have some level of experience or familiarity with the raw data. For example, referring again to the learning-to-drive example, familiarity with domain knowledge includes speed limits and playground zones. This is required so that the driver has experience with which data are useful for driving and which data are redundant (e.g., grocery store sign). Next, it is difficult to draw any reasonable conclusions from raw data without first reviewing the data and "cleaning" it where required (e.g., remove irrelevant data to the data set). Raw data can be unreliable, and, therefore, attempting to draw definitive conclusions will not yield useful answers. Issues with data, such as the source and the level of bias in the data, are important to consider with good decision making. Finally, computers cannot discern data quality; humans (with experience) must be involved in this process. Machine learning with algorithms is becoming more adept at correcting issues with the data.

Good decision making is built upon a domain of good quality data. Computers and humans are similar in that each requires a database of good, clean, raw data along with a mechanism for computing the raw data into something useful. How humans learn, store, and take risks impacts our data quality. Human decision making needs good data not flawed by our biases or with perspectives that do not represent facts. Good decision makers have the cognitive ability to learn quickly in new environments, often have less bias, and decision errors, and, therefore, there is reduced risk with their decisions.[1]

How humans build their own individual foundation for making decisions, in part, has to do with risk. Risk and risk-taking play a very important role in learning. A whole chapter has been devoted to the topic of risk (Chapter 5) because of the important role it has in making good decisions.

Steps to Becoming a Better Decision Maker

A good decision is based on knowledge and not on numbers.

—Plato

Becoming a better decision maker does not happen overnight; it takes time and experience. Practical steps are outlined in this section.

Education and training have been found to improve decision making skills.[1] Education can improve our ability to adapt to change and to think more critically. For example, a farmer with a formal education is more likely to adopt productivity-enhancing new technology in their farming work.[1] Post secondary education incorporates methods aimed at developing decision making skills that include critical thinking assignments, exposing students to a wide variety of problems. Incorporating case studies requires students to think more abstractly and draw upon the theoretical foundation taught during their post secondary education. This type of approach requires critical thinking (the ability to use facts to form a judgment). Good critical thinking improves problem solving and decision making, leading to better business, personal, and financial results. This critical-thinking skill helps people become more comfortable with ambiguity and the problems they may encounter in their jobs and life in general. Using the frameworks (Porter's value chain) and project management processes outlined in this book is intended to help you focus on important decision making criteria and give context to decisions.

Gaining a variety of experiences early in our careers will prove beneficial in later years. What might this look like? Jobs where a person rotates to a new (sub) function every 6 to 18 months provides unique exposure, as each has its own processes, strategy, and challenges. Ask your manager to assign you to an inter-functional project, as this provides valuable exposure to other colleagues and the key drivers and challenges of their function. Job shadow colleagues in other functions. Ask questions and seek answers. Take courses; most companies offer a variety of internal courses—try one every couple of months. Continue your education through post secondary and continuing-education programs. Source and attend conferences and events relevant to your career.

Staying in a role for a couple of "cycles" will provide an excellent growth experience. For example, having responsibility for a budget requires setting the budget for the subsequent year. During that subsequent year, receiving monthly financial statements that include a budget versus actual comparison will provide important feedback on how well the budget was prepared. Applying feedback from year one to a second year, and then following budget versus actual for the second year, will help build decision making capability (note: be sure to work closely with your finance partner to really understand your statements and the inputs into each line item!).

Within the workplace, another important method for learning is using company templates or processes required by the employer; for example, business processes or project management processes. While some of these might feel cumbersome or can slow us down in our jobs, they provide benefits for both employees and the company. There are literally hundreds of processes in any company, from how to order office supplies to filling out a purchase order, or logging into a portal to book annual vacation time or to note sick days. These processes provide a level of standardization in the workplace so that all employees are taking the same actions. Processes that are employed on a regular basis will be burned into memory and eventually become automatic. But from a decision making perspective, they serve an important role; they help us learn new skills and orient us to the culture and requirements when joining a new company. For example, goals are usually created when starting a new job. Completing the performance review process requires that these new goals be documented. The goals provide a roadmap indicating what is important on the job during that first year. Revisiting your goals at the end of the year will determine the overall success of your first year and should prove to be a useful growth and learning experience.

For employees in jobs that have higher predictability in decision outcomes and low variance in task, specializing in a role can make sense, argues researcher Epstein.[8] However, he argues that gaining diverse experience from a variety of domains is more valuable in today's economy. Because problems are more complex today; they, therefore, have less predictability in outcomes, and having a greater range of exposure to a variety of domains will build a more diverse foundation on which to make connections for solutions. Therefore, building a foundation of good data quantity, variance, and quality data should lead to being a more valuable employee over time. In essence, junior employees will benefit from being generalists and having exposure to multiple fields and multiple project opportunities.

One final reason we should care about becoming better decision makersis that your career, and in particular the money you will earn over your career, is highly dependent upon being a good decision maker. Early in our careers, wages are similar across industries and disciplines. However, it was found that wage growth after age 35 is much higher for workers in decision-intensive jobs, so long as they can exhibit the ability to make good decisions.[1] Research on decision making changes over the last 50 years found that life-cycle earnings have more than doubled during this period; however, our peak earning years have now shifted from our late '30s to our '50s.[1] This shows the time it takes to build the foundation for effective decision making and that there is a substantial reward for those who take the time.

Summary

Life is a matter of choices, and every choice you make makes you.
                                    —John C. Maxwell

While the average person makes thousands of decisions each day, most of these are done subconsciously and require little thinking or consideration. Companies are seeking ways to replace workers for easy and routine decisions; highly predictable and repetitive questions can be resolved with algorithmic formulas and automation. Meanwhile, the industry is rewarding people with the ability to make complex and multi dimensional decisions. For the decisions in our careers and relationships that matter, being a good decision maker is important to our success. Critical thinking and being a good problem solver are highly sought-after skills by industry.

Becoming a good decision maker can take years to build a solid foundation. A good foundation is built from factors such as a formal education and training. Incorporating useful tools (e.g., project management) and frameworks (e.g., Porter's value chain) provides a roadmap for decision making. Finally, good decision making is derived from people becoming generalists early in their careers because of exposure to a wide variety of issues. All of these build a foundation of versatile experience and knowledge to draw upon later in one's career. A final factor which is necessary to becoming a good decision maker relates to the topic of risk, which will be discussed in Chapter 5—Risk.

How is a good decision determined and who determines whether it is? A good decision at one company might be frowned upon at another. We need context for determining what a good decision is. These topics are explored next in Chapter 4—Strategy, Goals, and Measurement.

Application Questions

1. Discuss the pros and cons of being a generalist versus a specialist and how each contributes to a successful career.
2. Discuss how bias can impact making good decisions.
3. Determine how project management tools and processes can support good decision making.
4. Discuss how our work experience can promote value-creating project decisions.

CHAPTER 4

Project Strategy, Goals, and Measurement

Learning Objectives

- Understand the importance of company information as it relates to value-creating project decisions.
- Define how to make value-creating decisions.
- Discuss the importance of measurement.
- Discuss how to effectively measure supply chain partners.

Overview

Let's start this chapter with a short role play. Assume it is the end of the first year of employment for an employee (EE) working in a supply chain position. The employee and their manager are meeting to discuss the employee's performance over the previous year.

Mgr: How do you think you did this year?

EE: Great! I initiated a project to source a new supplier who is providing us a lower rate than our other suppliers. Second, I put a project proposal together for new technology that will enable us to perform some insightful analytics and learn more about our customers. I give myself a 5 out of 5!

Mgr: Really? I have given you a 2 out of 5. We are a low-cost-based company, which means we operate on thin margins and high volume. The new supplier ran us out of product three times and because you gave them exclusivity we couldn't turn to our other suppliers. We lost many customers this year because we had no product. Your project proposal for new technology failed to demonstrate where the savings would double the cost to implement. I am afraid you don't understand what it takes to be successful at this company.

There are many problems with this short scenario. First, and perhaps most importantly, goals should have been established when the new employee first started their job. All employees new to a job and a company should be made familiar with their goals so that they can manage their priorities and not get side-tracked with non urgent issues. Yet in the scenario, it appears that neither party sought clarity with the other for a full year. Unfortunately, this situation occurs more often than it should. It is both party's responsibility to establish agreement on what the employee's priorities should be for the year. Employees should be clear on what success looks like and how it will be measured.

The second piece of information the employee requires is what the company's priorities are (strategy and goals) and how these are linked to their own personal goals. This ensures that the employee understands how their performance, projects, and achievements help the company succeed.

Third, the employee needs to receive progress reports and feedback on whether they are achieving their goals. This process between the employee and their supervisor should occur on a regular basis throughout the year. Thus, any deviation between goals and actual progress can be discussed and remedied in a timely manner rather than waiting until the end of the year. The same applies for all supplier relationships. Good relationships are the result of clearly defined goals, and ongoing, open, and constructive feedback.

Recall the definition of a decision: "an irrevocable allocation of resources."[1] The output of every decision requires valuable resources and time. Because of this, all project decisions should be aligned with the company goals so that resources are used effectively and efficiently. We'll begin with a brief overview of the key information required to establish a company's goals, including the company's vision, its mission, and strategies. Next, we discuss the importance of creating economic value for the organization, and finally, we address supply chain measurement models, used for internal and external measurement.

> *Not everything that counts can be counted and not everything that can be counted counts.*
>
> —Albert Einstein

Vision, Mission, Strategy, Goals, and Other Important Stuff to Define a Project

Whether you are job hunting and considering an employment opportunity with a targeted company, or you are a supply chain professional wanting to initiate a project to source a new supplier, familiarizing yourself with the company is an important first step. For example, in the job performance scenario at the opening of this chapter, it was important for the junior employee to know they are working for a company set on keeping costs low. Knowing this at the beginning of the year would have altered the types of project decisions the employee would be making. They would have known the company would not be interested in fancy new technology used to perform analytics; that is, unless the employee's project proposal clearly demonstrated a significant cost savings analysis.

Most companies will host a collection of data points on their website. To become more familiar with a company, search through their media materials, including investor presentations. Presentations are typically held by the CEO and others in the senior leadership team. Read through the annual report and identify the company's goals, mission, and vision, and what key projects are being prioritized with capital expenditure. These types of documents will help build a profile of what is important to that company. All companies, whether public, private, non profit, or government, should have the same general collection. Some of these are briefly discussed below. There are also numerous sources of information external to the targeted company that can provide valuable information. Some might require subscriptions or a fee for access to company or industry information. For example, some of these sources could include credit information or industry analysis reports. Sources external to the company are not covered in this book.

The first important piece of information to note is the company's vision statement. The statement should be an inspirational ideal future state. A well-written statement should be clear and provide direction about what the company strives to become. A local grocery store used to have the following vision (which has subsequently been updated):

"To be the premiere shopping destination in the communities we serve."

The grocery store is known for having higher quality products and produce, albeit at generally more expensive prices. Their vision statement aptly represents this.

In contrast to the company's vision, the company's mission defines what the company does and its reason for existence. It should be written as current state or near-future state. Mission statements provide more definition than a vision statement. If both the vision and the mission statements are well written and studied together, they will provide good insight into the company, such as whether the focus is on quality, innovation, or the type of customers they serve. The following example of a mission statement is from the same grocery story:

"To provide outstanding service, quality products, superior facilities, and exceptional value."

This grocery store chain is well known for being community-orientated which provides consistently high-quality (higher cost) experience for the customers in their local communities. A wide assortment of cheeses, high-quality produce, customer grocery carry-out, daycare while shopping, and full-service gas stations are some of the amenities and services they provide. Contrast this with the opening scenario of the employee working at a cost-savings company; the grocery store stands for quality and variety and would be open to new products and services for their customer. Initiating projects in either one of the companies would be made on very different criteria. The mission and vision act as guideposts.

Another key data point is the review of company values. Values should be aligned with the mission and vision while providing insight into the company culture. There is growing research and evidence that values do in fact depict the culture of a company and what employees deem to be important. Common examples of values used at many companies include safety, trust collaboration, communication, excellence, accountability, or respect. While this list may be widely used across many companies and industries, how each company defines a word and gives it meaning is what makes each culture unique. At some companies, employees are asked to cite the values and have cultural reminders around the office, such as posters hung in employee offices or in the lunchroom.

Once the mission, vision, and company values have been defined, the company can create goals. These should be clear about what the company intends to achieve. Goals are written in the "SMART" format (i.e., specific, measurable, actionable, realistic, and time specific), meaning there needs to be tangible information associated with each goal. While this will vary for each company, short-term goals are usually 1 year in time, and strategic goals are 3 to 5 years.

The final piece of company information is a strategy. The strategy dictates how a company will achieve its goal(s), through means of a project. An excellent example of strategy definition is: Concrete expression of how a business intends to compete and win in its marketplace.[2]

The strategy should be orientated on what the company intends to do. However, note the word "intends"; the market is constantly changing, and companies need to initiate projects that align with customer, competitor, supplier, and regulatory changes. Therefore, the strategy must be fluid and flexible enough to evolve and maintain a space in the market. A strategy provides insight into how a company competes for a competitive advantage. Project goals must align with the strategy.

In my professional experience, I often see companies mesh goals and strategy. These companies may not understand the difference or importance of the two. Goal setting and defining the strategy are two distinct and different activities. The goals should be SMART and very tangible. Goals are "what" a company wants to achieve. For example, a goal might be a 5 percent increase in sales. Or it might be a Canadian company wanting to expand outside of Canada. The strategy is "how" they are going to achieve that goal. For example, if expanding out of Canada is the goal (of course, written as a SMART goal), the strategy might be through an acquisition or acquiring land and building new sites from the ground up (defined as a "greenfield build"). The final step is to initiate a project acquiring the land.

Once the company has its goals and strategy defined, three key additional activities should occur. First, corporate goals and strategy should be shared with all employees. Too often these are considered confidential. However, how can each function create a function strategy and goal without this information? Because goal setting should cascade down in a company, employees absent of this information are unable to set relevant and accurate goals.

Second, and last, based on the sharing of company's strategy and goals, each function should have their own goals and strategy. This ensures that primary and support functions collectively work toward the same outcome. For example, in the previous example, a company goal was to expand outside of Canada, perhaps to the United States. The human resource function should have a strategy addressing how they will manage personnel in an acquisition (e.g., move people from Canada? Retain employees from an acquisition?).

The supply chain function would also have a strategy in place addressing how it will acquire and move goods to a new U.S. operation (e.g., where to locate distribution centers). Their strategy should outline how the company will source and procure its products and services, and perhaps, more importantly, how it will get its products and services to market. This will help streamline supply chain project decisions. For example, if customer service is a priority, then same-day delivery would be in scope. However, if the company (and supply chain strategy) is more focused on being a low-cost provider, then the decision maker would be sourcing lower cost alternatives (unless the customer is willing to absorb the cost).

Most supply chain strategies focus on cost, time, quality, along with some other differentiators such as sustainability. The three noted, cost, time, and quality, are typically in conflict with one another. For example, it is difficult to provide overnight delivery for customers while also having a strategy of being cost-efficient. In the domain of project management, these three are known as a "triple constraint," suggesting it is difficult, if not impossible to achieve all three. Because of this, the supply chain decision maker requires guidance into which one of the three likely has priority over the other two, or conversely, which of the three is typically not part of a company's supply chain strategy.

Having well-defined company goals and strategy makes it easier for each employee to develop their own goals aligned with the company's and seek out associated projects. This ensures that all employees are aligned and in sync; collectively, all employees help the company achieve its goal(s). Further, this ensures every employee knows that what they do matters and contributes to the success of the company. This helps determine priorities which support value-creating decisions, covered in the next section.

Value-Creating Project Decisions

The goal for every single employee within a company, regardless of position, level, title, tenure with the company, or any other identifier, should be to provide value for their customer and, ultimately, for the company. The value should be defensible and measurable, and every employee should be clear on what they do, for whom they do it, why they do it, and how their value contributes to the company's success. If any one employee left their job, how would it impact the company? Would goods cease to be moved or tracked? Would relationships with customers suffer? In Chapter 1, the term value-creating was defined as a decision that expends a minimal number of resources, which is carried out in an efficient manner, and which creates opportunities or revenue, and ultimately profit, for a company. This section explores the term value along with the relationship with processes.

As it pertains to business, the term value is defined as having something someone is willing to pay money for. A person sees reason to pursue and obtain it. For example, we are willing to pursue and pay money for cough syrup or cold remedies when we are feeling ill. The product has value when we are sick, and conversely, very little value when we are healthy. For the company that created the cough remedy, their purpose is to take raw materials as inputs and transform them into an output that people are willing to pay money for. If the company can earn a profit through that process, then they have completed a "value-added" economic activity. If the public is not willing to pay a price for the product (output), which covers the cost of all inputs (raw materials, people, and so on) and transformation activities (manufacturing, distributing, and marketing) along with a profit, then the company has failed to create economic value for the firm.

Consider where your position resides within Porter's value chain: Is it a primary activity or support activity? Every employee in a company should be able to determine what economic value they create and what projects they can initiate to create new value. All projects must demonstrate how this is to be achieved.

The five project process groups (initiate, plan, execute, monitor and control, and closing) along with the nine knowledge areas (representing the 44 project management processes) were presented in Chapter two. These are employed as a means to progress work on a project. Similarly, business processes are used in the day-to-day operations.

Processes are sequenced procedures turning inputs into outputs until the goal or result is achieved. This suggests process require resources. Well-designed processes are intended to support decision making, align employees within a company, and, ultimately, deliver value to their customers. They should increase company effectiveness (provide value for customers) and increase efficiency (lower costs for the company). Good processes affect or pass through the least amount of people required to create the value and occur in the shortest amount of time. Poorly designed business processes cause slowdowns by passing through people or a function which should not be involved in the process or by building in cumbersome and unnecessary steps.

Processes have been included in this chapter not because the intent is to make everyone an expert at understanding the hundreds of them that exist at a company, but rather to underscore the importance of how companies create value and the complexity involved in creating that value. Each time a company's leaders adjust the goals and strategy aimed at increasing company value, the change is embodied in a project. These projects typically require a change to employee jobs, including the business processes they follow and what tools and resources they use to create value for the company. Let's take a simple example. Suppose the goal is to manufacture their products locally through an existing plant and cease outsourcing with a supplier in another country. The strategy might be to automate one of the company's local plants. Consider some of the changes and impacts for employees regarding the existing business processes! The distribution channel for inputs and outputs must change which include severing international supplier relationships. Then to automate the local plant, there must be changes to employee roles and how work is currently done. How value is created, who creates it, and how it will be measured all have to be adjusted.

So far in this chapter, the importance of a vision and mission along with other key data points which signal important information about a company, such as their values or safety philosophy, have been discussed. Next, company goals and strategy were reviewed. These indicate what employees should prioritize in their work. These data points can be strong signals to help you understand and identify projects that are important to a particular company. Third, processes articulate how work gets done in a company. Processes should be streamlined and indicate how value is added in each step of the process. Creating economic value is what keeps a company profitable. All these help ensure a company has a space in the market and can compete in the competitive landscape. Next, we turn to measurement. Measurement is required to determine if the project goals have been achieved and exactly how much economic value has been created.

Performance Measurement and Project Maturity

If you cannot measure it, you cannot control it.

—Lord Kevin

Everything can be measured. Some goals may be easier to quantify and measure than others, but everything can be measured.

—Denise Chenger

Performance measurement is used to assess the efficiency and effectiveness of a project decision. It provides a feedback mechanism indicating whether the decision taken provided value and achieved the goal. In order to create value, taking action with a decision requires using resources. Once it has been determined what is to be measured, the next step is to determine the process for measurement (or how it is to be calculated), who will do the measuring, and from what data source over a specific time period.[3] For example, if the goal is to open a new warehouse, then this becomes the metric. It would be measured against some time period (e.g., construct a new warehouse this year). Finally, the metric should be simple to calculate and clearly demonstrate the results.

Performance metrics should reflect the strategy and goals of the company and be aligned with customer expectations and commitments. For the supply chain function, metrics should align with the strategy and goals of the function and demonstrate how the function metrics support the achievement of company goals.

If it can't be expressed in figures, it is not science. It is opinion.

—Robert Heinlein

Measurement is important for businesses large or small, profit and nonprofit. It is a means of determining whether the company achieved what they set out to do. Measurement determines if the company created value and if so, how much. Each employee should be able to demonstrate the value they created for their company. Therefore, measurement starts at the individual level. Most employees, if not all, will complete an annual performance review process where manager and employee discuss what the employee did or did not achieve during the prior time period. Having clear goals and the ability to measure progress is often linked to increases in salary, additional compensation, such as bonuses or stock options, and advancement within the company.

Performance evaluation is an opportunity to demonstrate whether goals, such as safety, teamwork, financial, customer service, and so on, were achieved.

Learning occurs through the goal-setting process. This process includes having tangible goals and targets, a form of measurement over a specific time period, and the capability of capturing information through a feedback mechanism to solidify results. This process is intended to make us better decision makers. Ideally, it requires an easy-to-follow measurement standard, regular intervals of feedback, along with a supervisor capable of providing constructive feedback and holding us accountable.

One other important note on measuring employee performance: measure only that over which the employee has direct control. For example, suppose multiple people are responsible for the shared operation of a warehouse, but the profit and loss of the warehouse is assigned to one person. This would provide an unfair assessment for one person, as they would be held accountable for results that they can neither control nor manage. Further, the work of the other employees is not recognized, be it good or bad performance.

Once individual goals are established (along with how they are measured), employee goals roll up to the function level and subsequently up to the senior levels of the company. These results are then reported by the company to the greater community, such as through an annual report or a press release.

Typically, the finance function is responsible for capturing the financial results and disseminating throughout the company and to key stakeholders. Results can be viewed from a macro-company level or disseminated to provide each employee with their own results at the individual level. Financial results provide only one type of measurement. Other functions can be involved in the assessment and documentation of results, such as safety or meeting project deadlines and goals.

Measurement is used for benchmarking against others in the industry. And finally, countries are measured against others for productivity (directly tied to our wealth as a nation), sustainability, GDP, or other important global measurements. The next section shifts from defining measurement and how it is assessed to taking a closer look at how the supply chain team within a company can effectively measure function results.

Supply Chain Performance Management System (SCPMS)

A supply chain performance management system (SCPMS) consists of the performance metrics which are used to quantify the efficiency and effectiveness of the actual supply chain performance.[3] In order to build an effective SCPMS, recall that supply chain decisions focus on the resources and processes required to produce and sell a product or service from raw materials to their customers. Supply chain management is:

> *The systemic, strategic coordination of the traditional business functions and the tactics across these business functions within a particular company and across businesses within the supply chain, for the purposes of improving the long-term performance of the individual companies and the supply chain as a whole.*[4]

One of the goals of partnering with suppliers is to achieve a competitive advantage for the focal company. An SCPMS should have the ability to evaluate the overall effectiveness of each supply chain partner. Designing and developing a performance management system is a very complex activity and not germane to the focus of this book. There are several existing models which a company can adopt and adapt to their own business. The direction of this chapter is to provide background information on the purpose of an SCPMS and how it can be used to work with supply chain partners. However, measuring supply chain partners is far more difficult and will be discussed later in this chapter.

There are an estimated 16 different SCPMSs; here we review just two of the more widely used systems: the Balanced Scorecard (BSC) and the SCOR model. First is the BSC method.[5]

A BSC includes four distinct measures: financial, customer (aligning products and services that exceed customer expectations); learning and growth (sometimes called innovation); and internal processes (seeking means of efficiency and quality). The goal of a BSC is to take a holistic approach to measuring a company's progress by shifting away from the all-too-common spotlight on financial results. Companies who focus on short-term financial results and fail to develop a project portfolio for longer term competitiveness may fail to exist long term. Therefore, the model includes customer feedback along with promoting a culture of continual improvement through learning, innovation, and process improvement. The BSC is a simple, easy-to-use model which enables the company to link their long-term strategy with the four BSC levers. The four levers can be applied to individual goal setting, along with each function and company goals. Other benefits that include the BSC can be used company wide and are not specific to the application of supply chain activities.

The second SCPMS model is the supply chain operations reference (SCOR) model. While the BSC generally takes a company wide and internal look at measuring a company's results and competitive advantage, the SCOR model focuses on the supply chain activities (including their external partners) that help a company achieve a competitive advantage in the market. The purpose of this model is to evaluate the activities that achieve a company's customer demands through a "plan, source, make, deliver, return and enable" approach. This essentially evaluates the activities required of the supply chain partners in order to meet customer needs. Companies using the SCOR model can analyze their processes and goals, look at operational performance, and compare company performance against industry benchmark data. There are several existing industry best-practice metrics which can be used to evaluate a company's supply chain performance. This allows the company to compare its own performance against competitors. Performance can be measured based on reliability, responsiveness, flexibility, cost, and asset; projects would focus on achieving these priorities. Unlike the BSC model, because the SCOR model includes both company and supply chain partners, it is intended to measure both intra- and inter-company performance and enable communication.

Maturity Level

Maturity level assesses the capability of a company to continually improve. Maturity models are used for many different disciplines. For example, a company's ability to effectively use its project management processes to manage a project on time, budget, and scope, determines how mature they are on a maturity scale (typically four levels). A higher level of maturity for a company suggests that they have developed the capability to design and apply processes aimed at improving perform-ance in order to achieve a competitive advantage. Therefore, there is value in determining the maturity level of a company.

For a supply chain function, the maturity level indicates the function's ability to effectively use an SCPMS model in order to improve overall performance of the supply chain function and conceive of projects which further enhance the level of maturity. In this book, we examine the theory behind the effective use of an SCPMS to achieve efficiency and, ultimately, a competitive advantage.

Each level describes a level of effectiveness, resulting from the use and application of an SCPMS.[6] Level 1 is the lowest level and the least mature. Therefore, the ability to initiate and make improvements is limited. Level 1 indicates that the scope of change is limited to the function. Therefore, the function would lack the capability (maturity) to make any company wide changes required to become more effective. For example, in applying the customer category of the balance scorecard, reflect on the primary activities within Porter's value chain and the multiple company functions involved in the transformation process to produce their goods and services. If a company receives negative customer feedback, a level 1 maturity suggests the functions involved in the process would not have the capability to make widespread changes and improvements across the primary activities. However, one or each of the functions may be able to make changes that may or may not impact overall effectiveness and resolve customer issues.

Level 2 maturity indicates that the company is capable of inter-nally integrating across functions and developing tools to measure performance. It also suggests that the company is capable of balancing the demand and management of internal resources. Citing the same customer service example, the primary functions would have a higher level of capability required to execute the changes and resolve customer issues. This project would aim to determine the root cause of the issue(s) and where the issue(s) reside in the transformation process and then have the primary functions work together effectively to resolve the inefficiency and remove further customer complaints. The maturity model suggests that continual improvement (learning and growth) would actively occur across the primary activity functions to continually remove bottlenecks and remain efficient. Of course, the primary activity functions would include secondary support functions to be part of the solution.

Companies with a level 3 maturity have a higher level of capability. This enables the company to extend beyond internal optimization and shift into the external environment for improvement between customers and suppliers. This enables the achievement of shared performance goals. Finally, the highest level of maturity is a level 4. This level indicates the capability for inter-company collaboration and the sharing of a joint strategy between multiple partners.

Maturity level is relevant to decision making for the following reason: level 4 maturity requires each company in the chain to have the same level of maturity. It would be difficult, if not impossible, to execute improvement initiatives across multiple supply chain members (level 3 or 4) when an individual company may be ineffective in its ability to measure and improve its own performance (level 1 or 2).

Determining the Effectiveness of Performance Evaluation Systems

This next section provides an overview of the academic literature discussing the application and effectiveness of SCPMS models in practice. There is much to be learned from how well (mature) companies are able to improve their own internal processes (level 1 or 2) to achieve efficiencies and, ultimately, a competitive advantage. Further, how capable are companies at working collectively with supply chain partners to design projects aimed at improving inefficiencies in the chain thereby providing competitive advantages for those within the chain?

In the first study, researchers examined how the BSC criteria (financial, customer, learning and growth, and internal processes) could be used to measure supply chain performance. They goal was to examine both a company's internal effectiveness along with how it related to their supply chain partners.[7] The participating supply chain companies in the study were divided into four distinct segments: logistical firms, manufacturers, retailers, and a category they termed "IPOs" (defined as a sourcing company to support a parent company's need for parts and supplies).

The researchers produced a list of 15 metrics common to most industries (refer to Table 4.1). These metrics were assigned to one of the four categories of the BSC. Next, the researchers developed and administered a survey to the participants to determine whether each company incorporated some or all of the 15 metrics. In addition, the survey also asked the participates to rank each of the 15 metrics in terms of how important the metric was to their company.

The survey results produced some insightful discoveries. First, almost all companies included financial metrics, yet most companies surveyed did not include or have a strong focus on the other three categories of the BSC; learning and growth, and internal processes ranked particularly low. Recall one of the purposes of using a BSC is to shift away from a sole goal on financial metrics. The balance in a BSC

Table 4.1 Balanced scorecard performance metrics

Financial	Customer	Learning and Growth (Innovation)	Internal Processes
Return on investment	Market share	Employee satisfaction	Quality of service
Gross revenue	Customer retention	Employee turnover	Waste reduction
Profit before tax	Customer satisfaction	Number of suggestions implemented per employee yearly	New services implemented per year
Cost reduction		Money invested in employee training yearly	On-time delivery

comes as a result of having leaders in a company stress all four pillars. This approach requires employees to adjust their decisions away from short-term targets on financial results and into project decisions aimed at creating long-term value.

The next important result from the study relates to the level of importance each of the 15 metrics was to the success of the companies in the study and whether they were actively measuring the metric. For example, customer satisfaction: only 64 percent of the logistics companies and 63 percent of the retailers had a metric to measure customer satisfaction. Contrast this with IPOs at 88 percent and manufacturers at 74 percent. This result suggests that a logistics company delivering goods to their supply chain partners does not place a high level of importance on keeping their customer satisfied.

Another example from the learning and growth category is employee satisfaction. Logistical companies and manufacturers each ranked this low at 46 percent and 50 percent, respectively; however, the IPOs and retailers ranked this quite high at 79 percent and 71 percent. A final example is waste reduction, categorized within internal processes. Three of the four industry segments ranked this metric low with logistical companies at 45 percent, IPOs at 44 percent, and manufacturers at 57 percent. Contrast this with the retailers who viewed waste reduction as important, and 75 percent were actively working and measuring this metric.

While the study does not define the particulars of each of the metrics (e.g., regulatory requirement of a particular industry) or why certain metrics are, or are not, important to a particular industry, some broad assumptions can be made about the companies and industries participating in this SCPMS study. First, there appears to be no consistency with what each industry deems important or relevant to their success. For example, within the learning and growth category, the IPOs ranked employee satisfaction highest versus the other three segments, yet those same IPOs ranked employee suggestions lowest among the other three segments.

Second, what one industry deems to be an important metric as a goal to measure, their supply chain partner likely did not. For example, most retailers ranked waste reduction as an important metric versus the other three industry segments, which ranked this metric much lower. How can a retailer reduce waste and achieve its goals without their supply chain partners also deeming this to be an important metric? The retailer could be limited in how well they achieve this goal without their suppliers collectively working together to create value. This makes it somewhat difficult to determine what is relevant to each supply chain partner and, therefore, arduous to establish supply chain metrics with each partner company.

Finally, refer to the definition of "supply chain management." The definition notes the importance of supply chain partners integrating with a goal of creating a long-term competitive advantage. Each industry appears to have very different priorities and goals; how then can a supply chain create a common goal when the priorities of each member in a chain potentially are so different? What is important to one company or industry appears not to be as important to another.

The next complication related to an SCPMS, such as a BSC, relates to the maturity level of each company. Recall a level 1 maturity indicates a company is less mature and has a low capability of incorporating supply chain improvement processes. Therefore, a level 1 maturity company has a low capability of managing, measuring, or making improvements and would be challenged to make improvements beyond their sole function, and certainly not outside their company boundaries. Most companies have a maturity level of 1 or 2. This suggests that most companies struggle with making improvements across their own internal value chain. Therefore, developing performance management processes between companies as a means of improving the effectiveness of a supply chain is virtually non existent as there is no capability to do so.

Next, the researchers found that of the 16 existing performance management systems, only 10 of these are designed to be used with a company and a supply chain partner.[6] Further, only four SCPMS can be used across multi companies.[6]

Finally, there are significant variations between each of the 16 models. For example, one model may have a strategic application versus another may have a tactical application. The BSC is intended for internal use versus a supply chain application which are intended to extend beyond the focal company. Companies or industries may adopt a model for different purposes. With so many variations between models, it becomes difficult, if not impossible, to align any two SCPMS models with two (or more) companies. Therefore, the ability for two (or more) companies to be aligned and achieve mutual goals may be difficult in practice when each is using a different SCPMS than the others.

One final study looked at the effectiveness of SCPMS to determine whether supply chain performance is improving with any of the 16 SCPMS models. While the models were designed to evaluate supply chain performance, the research found that there is little evidence whether the models have been used inter-company and, therefore, little feedback exists on their level of effectiveness or whether the models are even in operation.[6]

The conclusion of this research? Choice of maturity levels, variations in how models can be used, different priorities and metrics between companies and industries all contribute to the lack of ability (or the inability) to develop project concepts aimed at driving efficiencies across supply chains with multiple partners. This lack of ability hampers the capacity to measure those efficiencies. An SCPMS makes good business sense for each company to work toward a higher level of maturity with a mindset of continuous improvement. Companies can initiate their own projects and measure the changes and effectiveness of their own supply chain but with "no one model that fits all," there is an inability to work collaboratively to develop these with supply chain partners.

The research noted in this section is now a decade old. More recent research continues to reinforce the earlier findings: multiple companies operating within a supply chain system have a limited ability to effectively measure the value created by the companies. Further, little empirical evidence exists about the actual impact of SCPMS on SC performance between two or more companies.[8]

If supply chain management is intended to create a competitive advantage by working closely with supply chain partners, exactly how can a company fulfill this objective? The SCPMS models are supposed to enable alignment between supply chain partners, yet the ability to execute this in practice is very difficult.

Practical actions for companies are as follows. First, each employee should be clear on their own company's strategy, vision, and goals, and how the company creates value in the marketplace. Every employee should know how their work contributes to that value creation. In addition, employees must be clear on their company's key strategic differentiator(s) versus their competitors. Having intimate knowledge of this information will provide guidance for employees and their decisions with supply chain partners.

Second, employees should use this information to seek out supply chain partners with values aligned to their own company while recognizing that no one partner company will be a total fit. Find ways to align key goals, and then create metrics and a method of measurement to determine how each party will adhere to meeting those goals. Build this into formal agreements. Remember, supply chain management is based on the idea of creating value for all members, even when those members use overly differentiated performance evaluation systems that are almost impossible to reconcile.[6] All members must provide evidence of the value created by their own company and how that value in turn creates value for the customer.

Creating Value—A Case Scenario

If it moves, it can be measured, and if it can be measured, it can be changed.

—Doug Pratt

Fast Transportation (FT) is a large national transportation company that moves goods from coast to coast. The goal for the vehicle maintenance (VM) function is to keep the company vehicles in good operating condition for use by the operations function. The vehicles require a large inventory of spare parts, which is held in centralized warehouses. The procurement function supports the VM function by sourcing and contracting with new suppliers. This ensures that the VM function can access those suppliers when parts need to be ordered.

Recently, the senior leadership team challenged employees across Fast Transportation to seek projects aimed at cutting costs and saving the company money.

One individual within the procurement function found a unique way to save FT a large sum of money. The current practice is that when a part is ordered from a supplier, that supplier will organize transportation and have the part transported to a designated FT warehouse. However, the procurement employee determined that if FT took on the role of moving a part from the supplier to an FT warehouse, the process could save the company a large amount of money. The procurement employee put out an RFP (request for proposal) and sourced a couple of logistics companies to ship the parts directly from each of FT's many suppliers.

This new process required an additional step from the VM function. VM still ordered parts directly from the supplier; however, in addition they had to contact a logistics company to initiate the movement of vehicle parts from the supplier to an FT warehouse.

It was not long before issues started to arise. Parts were arriving in torn boxes and missing parts, or boxes were lost. Suppliers were claiming that boxes were sent out in good condition and the logistics companies were claiming that they were not. The issues required additional work from a VM employee to complete a claims form along with photos of damaged boxes and goods. The new process took so much time that each region required a dedicated individual to trace package movements, submit claims, and discuss claims with supplier and logistics companies.

Soon productivity was down in both the VM and operations functions. Vehicle parts in limbo meant the operations function was unable to re-order parts. This impacted mechanics who were unable to work on vehicles until parts became available.

Frustrations began to run high for both the VM and the operations function. Why were they not consulted on such a change? Sure, one individual in the procurement function was deemed a hero for saving the company money and probably received a large bonus that year. However, that employee was probably unaware of the additional expense they caused other functions. Lost revenue, idle equipment, and changed job duties for many individuals all cost the company money; likely more than the savings from one bad decision.

Scenario Questions

1. Discuss the issues and narrow it down to one key issue (root cause).
2. Assess the maturity level of FT.
3. Discuss the role of the primary activities in creating value.
4. Determine how the changes to the existing business process impacted the efficiency of the business.

Summary

Reflecting on this short (but actual) scenario, there are a couple of key lessons to take away. First, if a decision is made solely on cost, it is not likely to provide the large savings payout anticipated with the change. Company goals should never be based on cost but rather on some other factor which aligns with the mission and vision. This will be discussed in more detail in subsequent chapters.

Second, any decision made within one function and in isolation rarely, if ever, will benefit the company. This demonstrates the low level of maturity existing within this company. Business processes can help provide exposure to how work moves from function to function with the ultimate goal of creating value for a company. For example, the order-to-cash cycle: trace the process from beginning to end and understand where value is created, where value is lost (and would your suggestion improve the loss or only add more complexity?), who is involved, and the time the process takes (where might there be roadblocks?). If your suggestion does not add value such as streamlining a process so that the customer gets a product faster, then the suggestion does not likely add value.

Last, recall the concept of change management from the project management section of Chapter 2 (supporting individuals adjust to the new changes). Let us assume for a moment that this initiative from the procurement employee was, in fact, a sound suggestion. People often reject ideas in which they were not offered the opportunity to provide input. Be sure to understand the challenges of other functions and involve key stakeholders to ensure the final proposed change or solution is solid.

So, what is a good decision?

Being good at decision making is being good at imagining the world you want to get to, the state that you wish to create. This idea of the future affects the decisions of the elusive present. If you don't have an idea of where you want to go, as the Cheshire Cat once observed in Alice in Wonderland, *then it really doesn't matter which way you go. Decision makers, focused solely on survival or domination in the present, miss this quality of the art.*[9]

Application Questions

1. Discuss the relationship between maturity level and value-creation.
2. Discuss the relationship between business processes and Porter's value chain.
3. Discuss three reasons why everyone in a company should be able to identify the value they individually create in a company.
4. Discuss why it is difficult to measure a value chain system.

CHAPTER 5

Project Risk

Learning Objectives

- Define risk resilience and discuss how it differs from traditional project management risk processes.
- Discuss how risk perception impacts project decisions.
- Describe the relationship between bridging and buffering strategies.
- Discuss how risk-taking helps us become better decision makers.

Overview

Take calculated risks. That is quite different from being rash.
    —General George Patton

As a supply chain professional, you are likely aware that supply chain disruptions have been increasing in frequency and severity.[1] This became especially prevalent with the supply chain disruptions associated with the COVID-19 pandemic. Prior to COVID, most people had never heard the term supply chain and certainly were not aware of the value of a global supply chain. COVID-19 surfaced supply chain issues that had been brewing and brought them into the front lines with consumers. Common consumer goods such as toilet paper and baking supplies were suddenly in short supply. However, COVID-19 has not been the only trigger causing supply chain issues; there have been other disruptions such as tsunamis, worker shortages, conflicts in a country of origin, and intangibles such as cyberattacks.

Other supply chain challenges include a decade-long trend for companies to outsource and to start offshore production. In addition, many products now have a shorter product life cycle, which increases a company's exposure to supply chain risks.[2] This has made the topic of supply chain risk management front and center not only for supply chain professionals but also for company leaders, industry, and governments.

The impact of a supply chain risk event occurring within one company is typically not an isolated event.[2] Events occurring at one company can disrupt a whole supply chain right down to the consumer. For example, vehicle manufacturing was hit especially hard with supply chain issues associated with COVID. Manufacturing and global movement of goods had been erratic throughout the pandemic, leaving assembly plants without the required parts. Retail vehicle dealerships were half empty, and consumers ordering vehicles had to wait 6 to 12 months (or more) for their new car. For the vehicle manufacturing plant, a new car cannot roll off the assembly line with missing parts. Global supply chains for many consumer goods, such as technology devices and vehicles, have been impacted. These unplanned events have resulted in financial, operational, and customer-relations costs.[3] Traditional risk management techniques, including those for projects, are proving ineffective, which requires companies to seek new methods to manage risk.

This chapter focuses on risk management: determining what it is and how we can get better at it as well as looking at recommendations for managing an increasing amount of primary activity risk. Risk also surfaces in projects. For example, weather can impact the construction schedule, or a contractor might be too busy to adequately service a project, or parts ordered offshore may fail to arrive on time. Risk cannot be avoided or completely erased from projects, operations, or within our personal lives. However, risk can very well have a negative or positive effect on a project or on operations. Only by actively managing risk can opportunities be identified and evaluated for value creation.

This is not a chapter about equipping you with a specific process for managing risk. This is because the possibility of a risk occurring is endless—whether we are outdoors, in our homes, in the workplace, or at a social event, we are all subject to risk. Further, this is not a chapter on how to manage risk in projects or in ongoing operations. The goal of this chapter is to learn more about risk and provide some tools to proactively manage risk so that when an issue surfaces in a project or in operations or on a project, we understand risk and have the necessary guardrails in place.

The chapter starts with a brief history of risk management and how it relates to supply chain risk management. It then addresses risk perception and how this relates to intuitive decision making, covered in Chapter 3. Once a foundation of risk management has been established, the remainder of the chapter focuses on supply chain risk management and resilience and how to integrate these into projects.

Risk Management—A Look Back

Much has been written about the domain of risk. The topic is relevant to every industry and to all disciplines. In the last decade, it has become a critical issue for boards and the senior leadership team at most companies. Banking and financial risk in the early 2000s brought new regulatory requirements such as Sarbanes-Oxley. Corporate social responsibility (CSR), which focuses on social and environmental risks, has seen increased scrutiny and attention in the last decade. A new risk comes with social media and includes the ability for customers and other stakeholders to publicly communicate their views on a company, their projects, and products. These developments have provided both an opportunity to promote a company and the opposite; they can create negative publicity. These are just some of the new and increasingly important areas of risk to consider and manage. The topic of risk has its own chapter in this book because of the increase in risk and the impact risk can have on both projects and supply chains.

The roots of risk management date back to the 1950s. Risk management started within the insurance industry and then soon expanded into the discipline of finance. It further expanded into the accounting profession, including the importance of audit.

By the 1990s, risk had become an important topic for corporate board members and the executive team. Boards looked to the leadership team to develop a risk management policy and required leaders to actively manage company risk. This led to companies implementing enterprise risk management (ERM) plans. ERM is an integrated process for aligning risk management with corporate governance and strategy. Having an ERM policy provides an enterprise a holistic view for risk decision making aimed at increasing a company's ability to achieve all operational and strategic goals.[4]

Fraudulent accounting practices led to federal audit and financial legislation, such as the Sarbanes–Oxley Act of 2002 (SOX) in the United States. This was government-mandated to help protect shareholders, employees, and the public. This demonstrates the increased attention and importance of risk management in the last couple of decades.

Most disciplines and professional designations will have their own standards and approach on how to manage risk. Supply chain management (SCM) has traditionally had a goal of making a supply chain more efficient and leaner, which, in essence, makes it more vulnerable to upsets and, therefore, riskier.[4] For the discipline of SCM, because risk management is typically more "outward" facing compared to examining company risks internally, ERM is not a term often used in supply chain risk management. Project risk management focuses on risk related to the project, which can include both supplier and company, among others.

Risk Management Tool—Risk Registry

A simple and straightforward method to manage risk while adhering to compliance requirements is with a tool termed a "risk registry" (Figure 5.1). This tool is widely used in industry, including project risk management.

The process starts with brainstorming and identifying what risks could occur in operations or within a project. Suppose a supply chain function has a project focused on sourcing a new offshore supplier. Brainstorming a list of risks could include country risks, currency fluctuations, lead time required for shipping products, language, and culture, to name a few. Each of these risks is then assessed as having a high, medium, or low probability of occurring. Alternatively, each risk is assigned a number from 0.1 (low probability of occurring) to 1.0 (high probability of that risk occurring).

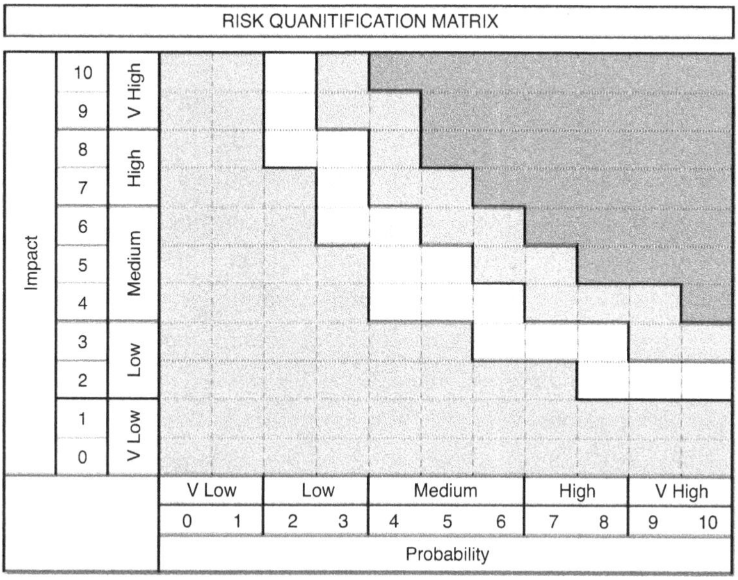

Figure 5.1 Sample risk matrix

Next, each risk is assessed for the impact that risk would have should it occur. The same low/medium/high or a number 0.1–1.0 is assigned to each risk. The impact of a risk occurring could include environmental damage, fatalities, financial, or company reputation. Revisiting the sourcing of a new offshore supplier project example, the probability of the country having a civil war break out might be very low, or perhaps a 0.1 or 0.2; however, the impact if the risk did occur might have a significant impact on the supplier's ability to produce a company's good. Therefore, this risk might be ranked high, or perhaps a 0.7 or 0.8 out of 1.0.

Once each risk has been assessed, the next step is to attempt to reduce, eliminate, or accept each one. The tool provides a numerical assessment by which risks that are ranked as both high probability (x-axis) and high impact (y-axis) can be critically assessed. For example, should the project be canceled because the risk is too high? Ideally, the project team should discuss, and a judgment can be made on how to best manage these higher ranked risks. In the example of pursuing a new offshore supplier, solutions to reduce risk might include sourcing multiple suppliers. Note that in this simple example, the solution may reduce risk; but, if the supply chain strategy is to be lean and cost-effective, this option may not adhere to the strategy and will fail to reduce risk. More of this will be discussed later in the chapter.

The risk matrix approach is a simple and straightforward method. It has pros and cons. On the positive side, any time a company actively thinks about and manages risk should be considered a positive initiative as it creates alignment and can help surface potential problems on a project. Second, populating a risk matrix takes little to no training. Because risks can be presented in a graphic form, it is user-friendly and easy to spot any high-risk issues. Third, the method can be used by any function or for any project and easily applied across the whole company. It provides a reasonably effective tool to proactively manage risk.

On the negative side, completing the risk assessment can be highly subjective—exactly how is low/medium/high or an exact number assigned? Consider if people are not accurate in their assessment of the risk and, therefore, the impact of assigning a ranking is not reflective of the risk. While this method is typically not completed by one person but more often populated and reviewed by multiple people, generally, only those risks assigned a high probability and high impact (dark shaded area) receive much attention and, therefore, risk mitigation. Take as an example: the probability of an airplane falling from the sky into a residential neighborhood is extremely low (perhaps a touch higher if the neighborhood is located close to an airport); however, should that occur, the impact would be catastrophic to people and property (probability = 0.1, impact = 0.9, total = 0.09). Note that this risk would reside in the low-risk area and, therefore, would not receive much attention. This demonstrates the limitation of a risk registry.

One final thought on the subjectiveness of the risk matrix method; I have seen colleagues attempt to quantify project risks to an exact number and believe their number to be the truth. How can we be certain about the level of risk when it is based on subjective information? How did we arrive at whether the number should be a 0.1, 0.2, 0.3, or other? There are very sophisticated tools, such as Crystal Ball and Monte Carlo, that take in historical information and provide actual probabilities. Again, these tools have their place and provide insightful information. However, even if the analysis were based on a very technical calculation, we must be open to the fact that these models can be flawed at the outset. The next section addresses some of the subjectivity behind risk management tools.

Risk Perception

What is risk perception? In essence, it is our ability to sense and avoid harmful conditions in our environment.[5] We can sense a lightning storm coming with dark heavy clouds rolling in. To manage the risk, we can move indoors for protection or, at least, move off the highest point in our surroundings! The ability to perceive risk and avoid danger is a necessary human survival skill. Much of our perception is based on experience—a child does not understand the danger associated with a hot burner on a stove, nor do they think about oncoming cars on the street and may run out to retrieve a bouncing ball. Our parents and caretakers help us learn about our environment. Sometimes we learn through experience. This is risk perception.

Humans and other living organisms can generally adapt to their surroundings and environment. Separating humans from other living organisms is our ability to alter our environment. This ability both creates and reduces risk.[5] Humans can alter their environment (and reduce risk); we can protect ourselves from harsh cold weather by insulating our homes. Or by installing and wearing seatbelts in our automobiles or wearing a helmet when playing rough sports. How can adaptation create more risk? Perhaps we drive more aggressively because we hold the false belief that a seatbelt will save us from all harm. Therefore, we have created a new risk.

If I were to ask people if they believed that there is more risk today than in years past, most would agree that there is more risk today. Further, these same people would state that the future will be even riskier than it is today. How are they assessing the risk today versus yesterday? And how can we quantify whether the future is riskier than what we are experiencing today? This is risk perception; that which we don't know feels "risky." This is exactly the research question that was pursued. A study was done in the late 1980s, and over 40 years later, we are stating the same thing: tomorrow will be riskier than today.[5]

The study also included people's perceptions about risk. It included a survey that listed 30 different risks. The list included police work, guns, smoking (cigarettes), nuclear power, and pesticides. The survey was given to four different groups, aimed at determining each group's perception of the riskiness of a given risk. Three groups included everyday people who had no experience in any of the risks. The fourth group were experts who worked with the specific risks. The three groups of laypeople were fairly aligned in what they deemed risky. For example, nuclear power, motor vehicles, and handguns were all ranked as 1, 2, and 3, respectively. Yet, experts in each one of the risks ranked the level of riskiness much lower—experts on nuclear power ranked it twentieth out of the list of 30!

What can we conclude from this study? Our perception of what is risky is based on perception of and experience with the topic. When experts judge risk, their response correlates with technical estimates. When laypeople assess the level of risk with the same activity, their judgment is based more on the hazards they perceive to be associated with the topic. For example, in the news, we may learn of a nuclear disaster. The report may include fatalities or an environmental impact. Yet we do not consider that this might be a once-in-a-lifetime disaster and fail to consider all the benefits associated with such a source of energy. A more frequent example is news that discusses fatalities associated with vehicles accidents. What we do not consider is the risk/benefit of transportation providing goods to our grocery stores and enabling us to move from point to point with ease. The news does not provide statistics such as how many people are on the road and how many kilometers the average person drives versus the number of fatalities. Without this important information, we may think driving is risky. A final note from the study on risk perception: we will accept risk from voluntary activities approximately 1000 times more than from involuntary activities. A simple example: many people are frightened of flying in an airplane. Why are people terrified of flying? In general, it is because we are not in control of the airplane (involuntary) versus a voluntary activity such as driving our own car.

Perception and acceptance of risk have their roots in social and cultural factors.[5] Our response to risk is heavily influenced by our friends, family, and community. Further, what feels risky in our environment might not feel risky in another. Recall that in Chapter 3, we discussed the five steps to becoming an intuitive decision maker. Level 5, the expert level, is the ability to complete a task in any environment. Using our driving scenario, the driver would be capable of driving on snow and ice, in heavy traffic, or on gravel roads. To any of us not experienced in any one of those driving conditions, this would be perceived as "risky." The topic of intuition also was discussed in Chapter 3; risk perception and intuition share a relationship. The more experience and expertise someone has in a topic within a particular domain of knowledge, the less complex (and risky) a problem will appear to that person.[6] Lacking experience in the domain can make something feel riskier than it might be. As an individual's perception of risk increases, they seek to decrease their level of risk exposure and vice versa.[7] Think back to how people perceived the level of risk associated with COVID; some people perceived COVID to be low risk while others perceived the risk to be very high. People's perception of COVID varied across a spectrum. Each person believed their source of information to be reliable and dependable. A caveat: I am not referring to people's specific medical conditions, age, or other highly valid factors surrounding COVID, in addition to the personal experiences we encountered, but, rather, merely providing an example referencing a personal perspective about COVID.

Our perceptions on a topic can be deeply held. If someone provides more evidence or information on that topic, it won't typically sway people to change their deeply held perception. For me, no one could convince me to go skydiving and jump out of an airplane or to go bungee jumping. Ask someone who skydives regularly and they will say the activity is not risky; however, I am unlikely to ever be persuaded otherwise. Our perception is influenced by information which aligns with our current belief as it will be deemed to be more credible. Further, that information will continue to reinforce our perception of that topic. On the flip side, evidence that is contrary to a perception or belief on a topic is likely to be dismissed, regardless of the source of information. It is difficult to move people away from their perceptions of risk on a topic.

Think back to our risk matrix discussed earlier in this chapter. The matrix is a graphical representation of what risks we have surmised; we cannot think of risks which are not in our domain. For example, I cannot imagine risks that people in other countries may encounter; I only know typical risks in my social and cultural environment. Next, once we think of a list of possible risks, a probability and impact number is given to each risk based on our perception of the likeliness of the risk occurring. Typically, the low/medium/high or number assigned to the risk is not based on a calculation (even if it were, what is the basis for generating the number?). This is why the exercise is flawed from the beginning. However, this exercise is useful to help consider a wide variety of risks and to think through the impact should they occur. This allows risk to be proactively managed. It is also useful for aligning people on the issues surrounding the risk in a company. However, it is not recommended to put too much emphasis on the results. There are additional methods of risk management and prevention to consider which are addressed later in this chapter.

Supply Chain Risk Management and Projects

Recall from Chapter 1 the definition of supply chain management:

> *The systemic, strategic coordination of the traditional business functions and the tactics across these business functions within a particular company and across businesses within the supply chain, for the purposes of improving the long-term performance of the individual companies and the supply chain as a whole.*[8]

Project risk management was introduced in Chapter 2 as "an uncertain event or condition that, if it occurs, has a positive or negative effect on one or more project objectives."[9] Next, we introduce the definition of supply chain risk management (SCRM):

The identification, assessment, treatment, and monitoring of supply chain risks, with the aid of the internal implementation of tools, techniques and strategies and of external coordination and collaboration with supply chain members so as to reduce vulnerability and ensure continuity coupled with profitability, leading to competitive advantage.[2]

The objective of SCRM is to reduce inter-firm vulnerability and ensure business continuity for supply chain members[2] and ensure a competitive advantage. In essence, SCRM is a means of enabling a company (and their partners) to create economic value.

Differences between the two risk definitions are that project management primarily takes an intra-company approach and is most concerned with risks that could impact project success. Contrast this with SCRM, where the focus is on both intra- (primary activities) and inter-company risk management, but with ongoing operations. Each serves a different purpose—project risk versus SC risk. Where the two definitions are aligned is that they both focus on achieving company goals.

Before a company can develop supply chain or project risk management processes, the first step is to define their own risk appetite and tolerance for risk. Each company has a different perspective on what is deemed risky; what is not risky at one company might be too risky at another. Employees need to make decisions that are aligned with the risk tolerance of their employer. This is discussed later in the chapter.

SCRM requires managing both internal and external risks. The internal risk management approach can be referred to as a "buffering strategy."[10] Buffering ensures business continuity by establishing safeguards to minimize company exposure to risk.[3] When collaborating with supply chain partners external to the focus company, the company is said to be exercising a "bridging" strategy. The goal of a bridging strategy is to maintain business continuity by influencing the external environment.[3] Both buffering and bridging strategies will be discussed in the next section. This will be followed by a section reviewing the models and means of measuring risk management.

Buffering: Internal Company Risk Management

Most supply chain literature overlooks the importance of the internal risk component and instead turns most of the attention externally on suppliers and customers.[11] Yet, researchers evaluated the sources of SCRM, citing internal integration as the number one risk to manage.[12] Therefore, the ability to internally integrate and make good use of external supply chain information is cited as the most critical risk for a supply chain professional to manage.[12] In essence, the ability to manage risks across the value chain system helps ensure business continuity.

A successful risk management program must first begin with company strategy and goals and any other important identifying information. The importance of this step is discussed in Chapter 4. Without this critical company information, employees may lack an understanding of where to prioritize their project decision efforts within the company.[3]

The next risk strategy is to ensure leaders provide clear, explicit, and transparent communication. This should also include the level of risk tolerance the company is prepared to encounter and manage with any project or primary activity. Unfortunately, leaders rarely communicate this. This results in employees making decisions that match their own risk perspective and align with their own self-interest rather than their company's.[7] Because risk perception is generally based on our own personal experience, employees who lack experience may be overly cautious and risk-averse, causing the company to lose project opportunities. Similarly, employees who have experience with the subject matter may be overconfident and not provide the necessary time, governance, and attention a project warrants, thereby exposing the company to undesirable levels of risk.

In the absence of leader communication, it is recommended that employees seek out other means of understanding the company's risk appetite, such as sourcing the company's enterprise risk management program (ERP), company policy, or the project management office for guidance. Alternatively, ask questions and ensure project choices and decisions are aligned with the level of risk the company is willing to accept.

Next, companies need to develop their own internal SCRM policies and processes. These should include boundaries and governance around the amount of risk a company is willing to tolerate.[12] An example of a risk policy representing the level of risk a company will accept is signing limits or capital spending limits for project (smaller amounts for front line managers versus millions of dollars for a vice president).

Recall our simple risk matrix introduced earlier in the chapter. Some companies assign risk to each low/medium/high section. A high-ranked risk might have a dollar amount assigned for loss of assets (millions of dollars) or equate to multiple injuries or fatalities. Any plausible risk in this zone might require a certain level of leader or board approval or, alternatively, could indicate that the company will not pursue projects or operations with this level of risk. Boundaries such as this help employees determine the level of risk the company is prepared (or not prepared) to take. Other examples of parameters might include whether the company is willing to pursue projects outside country boundaries. For example, conducting business offshore exposes the company to a higher level of risk (time, language, and so on). These examples help provide parameters for employees to guide them with their own risk management decisions.

There are two additional topics pertaining to internal risk management processes that are noteworthy. First is the capability of a company and its employees to effectively gather, understand, and use (exploit) information gained from customers, suppliers, and the external competitive environment and to manage the risk associated with the information.[11] This relates to the maturity level of a company in interpreting information and managing the risk associated with risk tolerance found in company governance policies (the concept of project and supply chain company maturity levels is discussed in Chapter 4). The higher the level of maturity, the more adept the company is in exploiting information used to reduce risk and make value-creating project decisions.

Second, companies need better methods of monitoring risk activities (particularly in real-time) and ultimately preventing risks before they occur.[3] Employees are not rewarded for preventing incidents. In addition, nonevents are difficult to track, determine a root cause, and measure. Therefore, without a process, employees will tend to manage risk as it occurs within their job. Typically, everyone is too busy to stop and examine how and why an issue was prevented. However, this step may help prevent future incidents, which would avoid impacting customers, such as delays in production and increased costs to the company. Again, this points to the risk management maturity level of a company.

Bridging: External Risk Management Process

This section provides relevant research and helpful information when working with supply chain partners. Supply chain partners have an important role in helping a company manage risk. It can be difficult to manage inter-company risk because of issues such as variations in each firm's operating model or project processes, combined with the quantity, complexity, and interdependency of supply chains and their configurations.[13] This issue is discussed in Chapter 4 in relation to the maturity level of a company. Given the potential impact on profitability and efficiency, along with the increase in supply chain upsets such as COVID-19, it is pushing companies to develop new means and processes to manage these risks. Research suggests that traditional supply chain risk management processes are proving ineffective in managing the inter-company relationships found in a supply chain.[1] Any company that can develop a method to manage risk with their supply chain partners can lead to a competitive advantage.

Bridging strategies consist of supply chain methods to influence the external environment and ensure business continuity for the focal company and, ultimately, for their supply chain partners. When done correctly, this helps minimize the company's risk exposure while improving the company's ability to better manage uncertainty in the environment. In essence, bridging strategies are intended to help capture information which is timely, accurate, and trusted. To do this, a company needs to create links to the external environment, which will gather relevant information and feedback for managing supply chain continuity and avoiding disruption.[3] This allows a company to be proactive and, ideally, ahead of any supply chain upsets. Links are any means of obtaining information from the external environment. This can include the ability to capture real-time information (project or operations); such as the status of a shipment in transit or a supplier manufacturing issue. It can also include proactive means to capture competitive information; professional associations and chambers of commerce are just a couple of the many examples.

Second, the company must develop and maintain close relationships with their supply chain partners, both customers and suppliers, projects or operations. Close, trusted relationships with supply chain partners have been found to result in greater information sharing. Information sharing includes the ability of partners to monitor their competitive advantage, then exchange information and conduct joint activities. This process has been found to provide advance warning of potential upsets and to avoid supply chain disruption.[11] Sharing of both strategic and transactional information, on a project or in operations, with trusted partners is required. The strategic information ensures partners know what is important and relevant to your company. This is then managed in the day-to-day transactional activities or for project planning and execution. A simple example: Canada has a highway that runs across the country. At present, there is a 3-year major highway expansion project underway causing a small segment of the highway to be closed for months on end. This forces traffic to be rerouted, causing increased volume and delays on the diverted route. Companies first need to capture this critical project information such as the schedule of highway closures. Next, supply chain partners working together closely can put plans in place to manage the road closures more proactively, thereby preventing supply chain upsets or increased costs associated with the diversions. For example, options for risk management might include hauling larger loads, shifting to rail or air, and rerouting goods from the opposite direction.

The final component of managing risk externally (bridging) is for a company to have the capability of analyzing data found through their links to the competitive landscape and trusted supply chain relationships. Feedback is an important component for improving goods and services along with risk prevention activities. However, exactly how companies leverage data to improve efficiencies, manage risk, and create economic value is not fully researched or understood.[14] Companies lack the maturity to translate data into risk management, improvement, optimization, and resilience, required for a company attempting to take advantage of opportunities or to reduce risk.[14]

To create a competitive advantage, the ability to receive information, assess it, and respond quickly and accurately to environmental changes has been linked to superior performance.[10] Most companies are now collecting large amounts of data. However, recent research suggests that they and their supply chain partners are still far from efficiently integrating big data into their companies.[15]

In summary, risk issues are constantly occurring in the external environment; the ability of supply chain professionals to interpret that risk and make good business decisions that are aligned to company policy and governance is deemed to be the number one way to manage risk. Most companies lack the maturity to prevent and proactively manage risk. As noted, having good policies and governance is a good start so that employees may align their decisions. Both buffering and bridging strategies are essential parts of SCRM best practices, and therefore, companies should have SCRM strategies both intra-company and with supply chain partners.

Project Decision Making and Risk

I can accept failure. Everybody fails at something. But I can't accept not trying. Fear is an illusion.

—Michael Jordan

To date, research has put more emphasis on risk assessment and risk mitigation (the ability to list risks which could occur and put a plan in place to reduce the level of risk) than on supply chain risk resilience (putting plans in place to absorb or recover should a risk occur).[16] In addition, rewarding employees for preventing problems has not been common practice.[3] This is mainly because it is difficult to track and measure that which did not occur.

If risk assessment is based on, in part, our perception of and experience with identifying risk(s), then this suggests that the models of risk assessment and mitigation may be flawed from the start. Let's take an example. Every decision requires data as an input. Often experience is our data source. But let's assume we will collect sales data and use it to make a decision (such as a project focused on expansion) instead of using experience. Determining which data to use requires our experience and judgment, so it is almost impossible to pull bias (judgment) out of the situation. For example, should we use 3 years of sales data? Should we average the data, or should we look at trends within the data? Should we use only the most recent year? Should we use data before COVID-19 radically changed our supply chains? Is the data before COVID-19 even relevant anymore, or has our business (and society) changed too much in those 3 years? Therefore, deciding which data to use requires a judgment. Judgment is not fact. Therefore, our model is somewhat flawed before we even look at the actual data. In addition, two people with very different experiences will view the data through their own lens and each conclude how risky something is.

Assuming there is inherent risk in everything we do, then none of us lives risk-free each day. Each person must accept a reasonable level of risk in order to function in the world. So too do the companies we work for. This is where goals and strategy come in; what is important to the company should be managed, measured, and monitored. This section discusses how supply chain professionals and their company move beyond traditional assessment and mitigation tools and frameworks and build resilience into the supply chain.

Resilience and Risk Management Models

Resilience is defined as a system's ability to absorb change.[17] Supply chain resilience is "the adaptive capability of the supply chain to prepare for unexpected events, respond to disruptions, and recover from them by maintaining continuity of operations at the desired level of connect-edness and control over structure and function."[18] When a company has a clear plan to manage or deal with business upsets, then any supply chain issues (projects or operations) causing the upset should result in a quicker recovery time.

The purpose of a resilient supply chain is to strike a balance between keeping high service levels for customers, balanced against controlling higher costs associated with ensuring business continuity and responsiveness. Contrast this approach to a lean supply chain where the main goal is cost reduction and efficiency. Either of these scenarios should demonstrate why having a clear strategy and aligned project goals impacts success! Let's review a simple example of a lean supply chain, and therefore, what low resilience looks like.

Suppose a company has one centralized warehouse serving all customers in a geographical area. Consider the many risks which could occur and impact the business continuity of the warehouse: flood or fire, road construction impacting the flow of traffic, snowstorm, and so on, Should one of these risks occur, causing a disruption at the warehouse and customers were not served, then as a result, the cost savings desired with a lean supply chain would ultimately cost the company money and, potentially, customers and reputation. Therefore, with the current configuration, the company has not established itself as being resilient due to the risk of disruption. Resilience provides for a level of business continuity.

The Boston Consulting Group[21] has measured companies that concentrate on risk resilience versus being lean and cost-effective. They found that in the long run, companies that establish themselves as resilient will outperform those companies that direct their attention on cost. There are additional costs to being lean which should be measured such as losing customers' trust and their business due to closures and supply chain upsets. Risk resilience planning makes good business sense. Project planning should aim to capture the current direction of the target company.

Components of a Resilience Plan

Changes in the marketplace occur fast and frequently. Therefore, a risk plan should be reviewed and updated regularly. Plans that sit on a shelf for years run a low probability of being effective.

Every company's plan will look different from another company's and is based on the characteristics of each company (goals, projects, and so on), the industry it operates within, their geographic location(s), and myriad other factors. There is no one-size plan to fit every company.

A supply chain resilience plan should start with a good understanding of the strategy, goals, mission, risk appetite, and enterprise risk management ERM plan. Any risk resilience plan that builds in additional costs to plan for business upsets or, conversely, is focused on being lean and removes additional costs from the business (with increased operational risk) must be clearly aligned with the company direction and risk tolerance levels. In other words, the plan must be aligned to the risk appetite of the company.

The next step is to understand the strategy and business goals along with how the primary activities create value. For example, does the business compete on speed? Understanding how the primary activities are linked to create value can shed insight into where vulnerabilities reside. This serves to provide guidance for project decisions.

Know what is important to the customer (and if something is important to the customer, it should be important to you and the company). For example, some grocery stores compete on price, and others compete on amenities such as carry-out groceries or on-site childcare. Others may compete on having a variety of hard-to-find products and carry products for people with certain dietary concerns. Only then can you safely identify where vulnerabilities and any redundancies exist and initiate projects that close these gaps.

In any supply chain, there will always be some vulnerabilities and some redundancy (i.e., excess cost), neither can be completely avoided. However, the goal is to try to identify where they may exist, think them through, and have a plan so that project goals are aligned.

To reduce the vulnerability or the redundancy, incorporate both bridging and buffering strategies. These strategies increase cost but are meant to reduce supply chain disruptions and smooth out issues. Buffering strategies within the company can include projects focused on changing the safety stock, regionalizing the business, and using multiple versus single source suppliers. Look beyond inventory strategies and include additional layers of the supply chain, such as logistics and distribution companies. Include multiple suppliers and leverage their market insights and information.

Along with buffering strategies, work in association with supply chain partners to develop bridging strategies. All relationships, ongoing or within a project, should be built based on clarity of your partner's goals and key identifying company information; for example, solvency, customer reviews, geographical coverage, to name a few key factors. The risk resilience plan should be represented and built into your projects and reflected in formal (contracts and agreements) and informal relationships with your suppliers and should include the following. First, performance metrics. How will you evaluate whether your supplier is meeting your needs and doing a "good job"? When a company is clear on their goals, these can be defined and captured within contracts with suppliers. For example, these might include event management response and responsibilities. What is their plan for supply chain upsets with their suppliers? Should they store your goods? Are they able to draw upon multiple suppliers or have multiple storage points?

Second, how much visibility does your company require with respect to where your goods are in transit, with both your suppliers and your customers? Do you require access to real-time inventory? It can be expensive and difficult for some industries, which adds a layer of complexity and cost. Determine a reasonable time window that provides visibility while reducing technology costs and demands. For example, real-time inventory with fluids in the transformation process is difficult to achieve (e.g., when is a grape no longer a grape but instead juice?). Therefore, will inventory levels once every 24 hours suffice? Determine the window of information required so that risk resilience planning can be done for upsets or issues. And in conjunction with the access to information, how will information be accessed? Will it be linked to technology (with good data?) or does someone need to pick up a cellular phone and call?

Next, having effective communication with supply chain members is necessary. Defining what it means to be an effective communicator, or having effective communicators, is important so that there is a process in place and expectations can be managed. Some hints to consider include: having a platform in which to communicate and share information; determining meeting frequency; agreeing on metrics and measurement for the correspondence and what level of granularity is required (e.g., do you need to know if something is backordered or just that a shipment is late?), and so on.

Finally, trust. Trust is a tough term to describe, and it has become a term thrown around too easily. Trust is based on the willingness to be vulnerable in a time of need. We must place confidence in another person or company so that we may be successful and achieve our goal. In other words, we cannot achieve our goal without them. It would be unwise to just hope they will fulfill their duty, but instead, trust should be based on something tangible.

Trust is not granted but earned in every relationship. It is built over time. To help establish trust, do background research on proposed suppliers; are they reputable? Solvent? Will they meet business needs such as geographical coverage or warranties? The list should be based on what is important to your company and how those needs can be achieved with supplier relationships. Build these company requirements into the contract. To prevent risk, negotiate and then document all expectations to protect the company while managing expectations. Trust is established over time and through experiences with suppliers. Supply chain upsets are likely to occur. The ability to pick up the phone and talk with a good supplier, discuss scenarios for a solution, and work to implement a plan are steps that build trust. Over time, they become a partner. Suppliers who are unwilling or unable to work together signals that the work was not done upfront when the negotiations were being carried out and the contracts were established.

One final suggestion to consider with a risk-resilience plan: a project which rethinks your entire supply chain. Companies have been re-shoring for almost a decade for many reasons: sustainability, time, and complexity. Moving offshore just because it is costly to manufacture locally has proven it is not always beneficial. The level of risk and complexity goes up a magnitude (not well understood) when we move offshore. Depending on your company strategy, industry, and business needs, re-shoring might be a wise decision. Start by doing some "what if" scenario planning; what are some of the issues that could impact your company? Time or distance to travel? Often it may mean a move to a new continent or re-shoring closer to company headquarters.

Taking Risks With Our Decisions

Do one thing every day that scares you.

—Eleanor Roosevelt

In Chapter 3, the five steps for becoming an intuitive decision maker were laid out. Moving from novice to proficient, or expert, decision maker is identified by key skills, which requires notable steps along the journey. In addition to the five steps, there are two components required for learning to occur and, hence, advance to the next level.[19]

First, research has found that the concept of risk-taking is an important component in learning and advancing through the stages. From our example of learning to drive in Chapter 3, taking risks does not mean the new driver (or any driver) can speed and take risks on the road. No, do not misunderstand the definition of risk. It means the learners must try the skill on their own and learn from the results of that experience. All new drivers are bound to make some errors. However, someone hovering over the learner constantly and telling them what to do will impede the opportunity for learning and for moving through the steps necessary to become a competent driver. The new driver must draw from their domain to make decisions needed to become a better driver. This is "risk-taking." Parents who make too many decisions for their children can hinder the skill of their learning how to make their own decisions. The same can be said for supervisors who make all the decisions for their employees and micromanage their work.

Here's another example of risk-taking that many graduates can relate to. Sometimes a student will ask the instructor for examples of student papers from previous semesters. It is understandable that a student wants to review papers to understand what an "A" paper looks like so that they know what work is required to achieve a similar grade. I personally believe it is important to set a standard and share this with students so that everyone is aligned on the end goal (the importance of goal setting was discussed at the start of Chapter 4, pertaining to an employee meeting with their manager to discuss the year in review). It is a very important step to align manager and employee. However, this is the value of a course outline, a rubric for the assignment (establishing priorities and goals), and being open to discuss obstacles and progress toward completing a project. Providing previous examples of papers almost negates the learning. Why? Because unfortunately, students tend to copy almost everything, including the font used, and then anticipate a good grade. But the content within may or may not meet the objectives. It is the instructor's intuition that can articulate the learned experience of the student(s) and, therefore, the risks they took. Providing previous examples only serves to hamper creativity and, therefore, limit learning. Risk has not been taken, which means learning is limited.

I am always doing that which I cannot do, in order that I may learn how to do it.

—Pablo Picasso

The second important precondition to learning a skill is that the person must understand the consequence, good or bad, of the decisions they make and take responsibility for their decisions. For example, if a person merges onto the freeway much slower than the current speed of other drivers, those drivers will have to step on their brakes and may even honk their horns at the merging vehicle. They honk because the driver has interrupted the current pace of the freeway drivers and may have come close to causing an accident. If the slow driver responds by honking their horn back, thinking the other driver is a jerk and a bad driver, then they will have failed to understand the consequence of their decision. If we rationalize the situation and put blame on others, our ability to learn a new skill is limited. To become better at decision making, we must think through the consequences of our decisions. We must reflect on the situation and be open to the impact of our actions on the situation. For example, a more accurate reflection of a poor merge scenario could look like this: "whoops, maybe I was going a little too slow and people had to apply their brakes, next time I will have to watch the speed of cars more closely."

Building a foundation is important, both in an academic setting and early in our careers. Having instructors who provide constructive feedback on assignments, or who inform students of resources to help them, goes toward building that foundation. In the workplace, receiving regular feedback from our direct supervisor, colleagues, customers, and others plays an important role in becoming a better decision maker. When we start our careers in a decision-intensive occupation, we do not have a foundation of experience to draw upon. However, varied experience and the ability to learn from that experience build a domain where later in our careers the reward is much higher. Does education help with that foundation? Many studies support this.[20] For example, one study looked at educated farmers and found they were more likely to adopt productivity-enhancing new technologies. The paper notes that education improves our ability to adapt to change. Adaptation suggests that we take in information and make good decisions to increase our chances of long-term survival.

Don't be too timid and squeamish about your actions. All life is an experiment. The more experiments you make the better.
—Ralph Waldo Emerson

Summary

In the end, risk is always all around us; we cannot avoid risk. How we manage it and let it influence projects is the decision. Risk is highly related to our experience and perception about what we deem to be risky. In the workplace, we need to align our risk perception to company goals and strategy along with the company's risk policies. And leaders must help communicate the risk tolerance of the company. In the absence of these, supply chain professionals will apply their own risk perception to make supply project decisions which may not represent their company.

Over time, companies which are risk resilient versus lean have been found to produce more value. Risk resilience projects which consider the value chain system will provide both tangible and intangible benefits for both the company and the system. This requires developing buffering and bridging strategies which are aligned with company risk tolerance and policies and that ensure project decisions are being made with an appropriate level of risk and business continuity.

Application Questions

1. Discuss how can we effectively use buffer and bridging strategies to manage risk in projects or in operations.
2. Consider where you may have bias in how you manage risk in a project, in your job, or in your life and why it's there.
3. It was demonstrated that a risk registry may be a flawed tool from the start, discuss how you could use a risk registry to effectively manage project risk.
4. Discuss how Porter's value chain can be used to support the risk management process.
5. Provide methods to effectively measure risk.

Making Value-Creating Supply Chain Project Decisions

CHAPTER 6

Make or Buy Project Decisions

Learning Objectives

- Define the strategic and tactical reasons for outsourcing.
- Understand why make or buy decisions are made.
- Apply criteria to a make or buy decision.
- Select appropriate criteria with which to conduct a make or buy decision.
- Use project processes to conduct a make or buy decision.

The important thing about outsourcing or global sourcing is that is becomes a very powerful tool to leverage talent, improve productivity and reduce work cycles.

—Azim Premji

Overview

Is it more economical to make a product or service within a company or to go to the market to purchase it? I have been asking students that question for years, and the answer is always the same: about half believe it is more economical to make the product, and half believe it is more economical to go to the market. Can they both be correct?

It would be difficult to think of any one company that makes everything they sell to the customer. A bicycle manufacture purchases the gears, tires, and other bike parts from trusted suppliers. Laundry soap manufacturers purchase the scent and other ingredients. The average vehicle has more than 10,000 parts that are assembled at a plant, but most of those parts are manufactured by hundreds of suppliers.

Exactly which goods or services are made and which are outsourced is usually a strategic choice made by the leaders of a company. For the person conducting a make-or-buy supply chain project decision, there are a few key responsibilities. First, the project manager and the project team should understand the strategic reasons for conducting a make-or-buy decision. Second, they should understand how their function and the company create value so that they can incorporate this decision making criterion when making a value-creating make-or-buy decision. Failure to fully comprehend both the first and second points can lead to unintended losses (financial and knowledge) along with introducing risks such as operational upsets.

Employees who are in a supply chain role should constantly evaluate the market for suppliers who can fulfill product and service needs for their company. Make-or-buy decisions should never be a one-time event. This is because the market is constantly evolving with changing customer needs, competitors introducing new projects, and new suppliers entering (or exiting) the market and offering new products or services. In addition, the focal company will be adjusting their strategy and evolving in response to a changing market. Therefore, these employees should be scanning the competitive landscape and analyzing the goods and services offered, including where they can be sourced, evaluating quality of vendors, time to acquire, cost, along with other important criteria in order to be aligned with the company direction. The data should be evaluated and compared to existing supplier data. This chapter provides an overview of how to conduct make-or-buy project decisions.

Defining "Make or Buy" Project Decisions

Consider make-or-buy decisions versus outsourcing versus vertical integration. Academically, we could argue that there are distinct differences between each of these terms. However, the literature also suggests that these terms are one and the same and can, therefore, be used interchangeably. Following a brief introduction of these, the term we use in this chapter will be "make-or-buy."

In Chapter 1, the term value creation is discussed. Two competing companies within the same industry can create economic value for their company in substantially different ways. How each company creates value varies and is dependent upon how each builds their individual value chain. A value chain was defined in Chapter 2 (the set of discrete activities that must be accomplished to design, build, sell, and distribute a product or service).[1] Understanding the term is important in identifying whether and which components of a value chain are held within a company, and which, if any, is managed external to the company. For example, a golf course might contract with a golf pro who is not a direct employee of the golf course, or the restaurant at the golf course may be owned by a separate entity. Companies must decide which components of the value chain they want to be directly involved with and how they want other companies to perform these on their behalf.

Sourcing is the process of finding a company that can effectively fulfill a company's outsourcing work scope. Outsourcing refers to the "act of transferring work to an external party."[2] It requires "the transfer of factors of production, the resources used to perform the work and the decision rights, or responsibilities for making decisions."[2] Outsourcing is the result of a make-or-buy project decision. It is a general term used to reflect a myriad of different arrangements between a company and a supplier; each having financial and strategic risks and advantages.

While companies have always had suppliers, outsourcing was only recently considered a strategic initiative. The initiative of outsourcing originated in the 1950s but did not become a popular endeavor for decades.[3] In the 1980s, outsourcing became a means for a company to offload noncore activities, such as information technology (IT). This approach allowed companies to focus key resources on the activities the company considered to be critical. Outsourcing originally began as a method to reduce costs. However, an unexpected outcome was that those companies who were first to outsource found that they were building stronger and more trusting relationships with the outsourced company. It was found that the early adopters of this initiative built new skills, competencies, and market knowledge.[3] Technology eventually enabled the outsourcing initiative by allowing companies to share information more easily and frequently.

While outsourcing originally focused on shifting noncore activities out of the company, at present, it includes moving primary activities within the value chain out to a supplier. Reasons for outsourcing have also expanded from a cost-saving endeavor to now include "strengths, flexibility, information security, loss of management control, labor unions and morale problems, vendor's service quality, market maturity,"[4] and other company specific reasons. Evaluating these reasons is covered later in this chapter. But first, background information aimed at providing an understanding of how and why to establish an outsourcing relationship is the focus of the next section.

A seminal study on outsourcing was produced just over a decade ago.[5] The researchers interviewed executives from a wide range of industries and included companies of various sizes. The goal was to study and learn about the executives' outsourcing initiatives. Insights from the interviews are laid out in this section. (Note: I highly recommend that readers source this paper (Gunasekaran et al) along with Sanders et al.'s paper to fully understand and appreciate outsourcing decisions and their framework briefly described in this section).

Outsourcing provides an opportunity to tap into unique skills not found within the company, and this can help the company gain a competitive advantage not found in the marketplace. Three reasons were cited by the leaders as their reason for outsourcing.[5] First, for financial reasons, outsourcing focused on reducing costs, including labor and production costs, along with an ability to increase revenue. Note, however, that the leaders found that they had not calculated the total cost of utsourcing but instead had focused on the new cost per unit associated with the endeavor. We will explore this concept in this chapter. In addition, leaders found that focusing on reducing costs was a short-term approach that could easily be replicated by competitors.

The second reason for outsourcing included a resource-based objective. This option could help give a company, lacking in specific expertise, the ability to find these resources in the market through outsourcing. This approach could help a company keep pace with regulatory and technological changes. The third and final reason was for obtaining strategic objectives. Outsourcing specific functions (or subfunctions) enabled the company to internally focus on specific expertise for a competitive advantage.

The researchers developed a framework to help readers visualize the findings.[5] The framework has two key categorical dimensions. One dimension was titled "scope" and was defined as the degree of responsibility assigned to the supplier. The greater the scope (or responsibility) outsourced to a supplier, the more that supplier would control the task. The other dimension was titled "criticality," defined as the degree to which the task was a primary activity of the owner company. Recall Porter's value chain where he defines a "primary activity" as a function being directly involved in producing the good or service. Therefore, an outsourced primary activity has a higher criticality than an outsourced support activity.

Tasks with low criticality and low scope are more transactional and typically require less effort to manage. As the outsourced activity increases in both scope and criticality, the exchange between the two companies shifts from being a contractual one to more of a relationship-based one. Outsourced activities which are high in both scope and criticality increase the level of risk to the focal company. This approach naturally requires a significant resource investment, including time, processes, and financial. This is necessary to build and maintain trust and commitment between the two companies and, ultimately, reduce risk and increase the benefit of outsourcing.

Next, here are additional definitions and notes related to outsourcing. First, "plural sourcing" refers to simultaneously insourcing and outsourcing an activity. Second, although not fully discussed in this chapter, variations of make-or-buy decisions exist, including strategic alliances and joint ventures, to mention two. Automation has also been suggested as another variant method of the make-or-buy decision. Finally, for good reason, make-or-buy decisions are one of the most researched topics in the supply chain domain.[6]

One final term relevant to this topic is "logistics management," which is defined as:

The process that plans, implements, and controls the efficient, effective flow and storage of raw materials, in-process inventory, finished goods, services and related information from the point-of-origin to the point-of-consumption (including inbound, outbound, internal and external flows) in such a way as to meet the customers' requirements cost-effectively and ensure that the current and future profitability are maximised.[2]

Logistics management is relevant to the make-or-buy discussion as this holds an important position within a company's value chain; goods and services cannot be effectively produced without careful consideration of how they are moved and stored. Logistics is frequently outsourced and not given the same strategic consideration by leadership as other value chain components.

In summary, make-or-buy decisions can be defined as projects focused on the decision making process of whether to produce intrafirm or have an external company make the good or service. These decisions can be very simple and straightforward or can be very strategic and complex, such as outsourcing an entire primary function or activity for a company. The process will be explored more in the Make-or-Buy Decision Making Process section. The term outsourcing typically refers to the actual process of having an external company produce the good or service. It is the term most often associated with the activities of supply chain professionals. While supply chain professionals often provide critical input into make-or-buy decisions, the ultimate decision whether to outsource typically belongs to the leadership team with input from the relevant primary function holder(s). This would normally be the project sponsor or the steering team evaluating the recommendation provided by the project team.

The next section focuses on the criteria used to make a make-or-buy decision. Following this, the project management decision making steps to making a make-or-buy decision are laid out.

Criteria for Conducting a Make or Buy Project Decision

Make or Buy: Is There a Lower Cost?

Let's start this section by addressing the cost aspect of make-or-buy decisions with a simple example. Years ago, I worked for a downstream oil and gas company. The transportation VP was responsible for ensuring all the retail gas stations had fuel in the tanks and available for sale to customers. Fuel was delivered by truck to each of the gas stations usually once or twice per week. The company at that time maintained a plural sourcing activity where the bulk of the trucks were owned internally by the company and a portion of the delivery was outsourced to a truck delivery company (which also delivered fuel to competitor gas stations). The VP wanted to switch that scenario to a 90 percent outsourcing activity. Consider all the costs to my company that were involved in fuel delivery: trucks in good operating condition, drivers to drive the trucks, service bays and mechanics to repair the trucks, truck bay for washing dirty trucks, vehicle insurance, training programs; the list goes on and on. Next, consider all the advantages of housing the activity internally with a "make" decision: flexibility, expertise, better customer service for the gas stations, and brand recognition ("free" advertising) of trucks on the highway. Now think about outsourcing most or all these activities to an external logistics company; after all, they should be experts at fuel delivery since this is their core business. This should indicate that they would have more flexibility than my company because they are also servicing competitors. As for the expense issues, don't they have the same costs as my company would? Don't they have the same trucks and mechanics, wash bays, drivers, and training programs too? Therefore, my company's internal costs to maintain a fleet of trucks should be similar to the internal costs of an outsourced company. So why outsource? What are the criteria for conducting a make or buy decision? How can we decide whether that activity should be insourced, outsourced, or remain a plural activity?

This simple example should provide a couple of early insights into the criteria for conducting a make-or-buy decision. First, the external trucking company would have an abundance of trucks, drivers, and other essential assets and experience that should provide some level of economies of scale. Second, because delivering fuel is the outsourced company's key operations activity, it is anticipated that they would be efficient at delivering fuel. Finally, let us address the profitability issue. Would we pay more to the outsourced company because they want to make a profit? Not necessarily. Think about the outsourced company's costs to operate the trucks versus our costs internally. One could argue that the outsourced company would be cheaper because they are experts. However, someone else would argue that it is cheaper to obtain the service internally because the internal function does not wish to make a profit. However, this is not typically true—the internal function will absolutely want to make a profit! (Be aware—achieving or exceeding the budget is usually associated with employee bonuses—and who doesn't love a big annual bonus?). That cost is prenegotiated between two functions (logistics and retail) and is called a "transfer price." Vertically integrated companies "transfer" the good or service from an upstream to a downstream division.

The transfer price becomes an internal price to negotiate between the two functions. However, the internal transfer price should be reasonably competitive with market prices. In other words, regardless of whether a function purchases products external to the company from a supplier or from a function within their own company, the two prices should be competitive. Note, however, the quality and value of both internal and external suppliers should be of similar value. Although make-or-buy decisions are strategic initiatives and require careful evaluation, companies should be constantly evaluating their internal resources and capabilities versus those found within the marketplace.

The last point to address on this short scenario is why the VP wanted to outsource over 90 percent of the fuel delivery business. Why this number? The short answer is there was no specific reason I was given to arrive at this number. Clearly, there are costs and benefits with this type of approach, some of which will be explored within this section and some addressed with questions at the conclusion of this chapter.

Tactical Versus Strategic Sourcing—A Continuum

Make-or-buy decisions can be very easy and straightforward. A simple example: my parents used to own and operate a golf driving range. They bought brand-name confectionary products, including soda pop and snacks, to sell to customers at the driving range. Alternatively, they could have made snacks and sold them. Making the snacks would have required that they purchase and maintain kitchen equipment, track expiry dates on the snacks for product safety, obtain licenses to handle food, and consider many other issues, such as their time. Baking snacks was not a value-creating activity my parents wanted to pursue for many reasons. First, it would distract from the ongoing operations of the driving range, which is the key focus of the business. Second, confectionary can easily be sourced and purchased from local grocers or wholesalers and delivered to the site for an additional cost. Third, although people like home-baked goods, most customers readily identify with brand-name products such as Coke or Pepsi. Finally, confection-ary sales made up approximately 1 percent of their total sales; this confirms customers don't go to a driving range to purchase fresh baked goods. This indicates baking and producing goods is not a value-creating activity. Brand-name companies can do this more efficiently. This simple example serves to provide a straightforward, nonstrategic make-or-buy decision.

Two brief examples of make-or-buy decisions have been discussed. These included buying snacks for a golf driving range and whether to distribute fuel with company-owned trucks or with a supplier who specializes in fuel delivery. However, most of these decisions are far more complex. A poorly thought-out decision can place a business under considerable risk. A bad year of financial results should not instigate a make-or-buy decision. While cost is always a factor in a make-or-buy decision, any decision made solely on cost is almost guaranteed to cause the company to perish.[6]

Make-or-buy decisions can be thought of on a continuum where the very tactical (and relatively simple to make) are on one end, and the strategic (and highly complex) are on the other end of the contin-uum. The driving range example is very tactical. While the snacks are identified as a primary activity for the driving range business (because they generate revenue), customers are not going to the driving range for them. Consider additional criteria about defining whether to make or buy the snacks. First, snacks such as pop and chips can be found almost everywhere (almost a commodity). We could state that they have stable demand (e.g., not a seasonal product). They are a short-term transaction (it is not wine where it will take years to produce and potentially sell). Snacks are made as a one-time purchase (even if they are purchased every week), meaning that after-sales support is not required. The transaction can be conducted with low or no communication, and an ongoing relationship with the supplier is not required. Where the chips or pop is purchased is not particularly relevant as the product or service can be found from multiple suppliers. These types of decisions tend to be made more on cost, which also makes them low-risk decisions as product or service stability tends to be stable.

On a continuum, while fuel delivery is tactical, it is slightly more strategic for a couple of reasons. First, for the retail fuel store, fuel delivery is a component of inbound logistics. This makes it a primary activity; the store needs fuel in order to sell it and generate revenue, but *delivering* fuel is not a revenue-generating activity for the retail store (for the retail business, it was considered logistics management). It is a primary activity for the supply function and part of the overall company operations. (This suggests that the impact of the final decision should be considered: what happens in one function can negatively impact another and determines the total impact to the company prior to making a final decision!)

Second, consider the scope and criticality of the activity. The scope, or responsibility, for fuel delivery can be managed internally or contracted to an outside distributor (high scope). The criticality is low to medium. In general, fuel delivery is a very predictable and easily scheduled activity. Having a good supply contract that captures the key requirements of the retail business and then monitors the requirements is essentially the extent of the relationship between buyer and seller.

Decisions that are more strategic require more analysis. The process begins with a strong understanding of company strategy, the product or service, and how the primary activities generate revenue. Additionally, knowing the core competencies of the company and how these create value will help provide context for conducting a make or buy decision. Note that core competencies that directly contribute to creating economic value are rarely outsourced. Second, industry information and knowledge about the industry the company operates within are also necessary.

As it relates to make-or-buy decisions, the Resource-Based View (RBV) of a company is an important concept to understand. RBV examines the different resources and capabilities each company possesses and how managers can bundle these to create diverse combinations for a competitive advantage in the marketplace.[1] Companies that have resources that are valuable and rare, and which develop unique, firm-specific competencies, can outperform competitors.[1] RBV can be used to explain how companies that capture value in their processes, and develop a means to exploit it, may create value so long as that value exceeds the cost to collect, manage, and analyze it.[7]

Unique combinations of company resources, including physical resources (infrastructure), company resources (recipes, raw data), and human resources (analytics skills or knowledge), can produce superior results when they are inimitable. Identifying, understanding, and classifying how companies develop their resources into core competencies is necessary in order to manage risk and create value. Each company can create economic value through their unique combination of resources, along with how they use those resources to produce goods and services within their value chain. Being clear on what the core competencies are at each company can help provide insight into which activities should reside within the company and which could be outsourced. Carefully consider whether an activity supports a core competency (or *is* a core competency) as outsourcing the activity might impact the competency and, in turn, the business and value creation.

Evaluating an outsourcing opportunity that is more strategic indicates a desire to assign increased scope and criticality to a supplier. An increase in criticality is associated with a primary activity, which can indicate a core competency that could end up residing with a supplier. Reasons why a company might pursue this option are varied, starting with what problem the company is trying to solve.[5] For example, perhaps there is a significant capital cost required so that the company can remain competitive with a competency, and therefore, the company may instead choose to outsource the activity. Or perhaps the company might partner with an industry leader who can perform it more effectively. These are two reasons why it might be a good idea to outsource a core competency.

Tactical decisions require a low level of communication and low to no ongoing relationship with the supplier, such as buying snacks and pop from a supplier for the golf driving range. However, as the scope and criticality increase with strategic outsourcing, so too does the level of risk.[5] Unlike tactical outsourcing decisions, outsourcing a primary activity will require ongoing additional resource requirements for both the company outsourcing it to the supplier. Strategic decisions require a commitment to communicate with the supplier and are more collaborative and relationship-based: this is required in order to establish and maintain trust between the two companies. However, this relationship can result in a mutual benefit for both companies and may help to create a new competitive advantage for both the company and the supplier. Strategically, building relationships with suppliers, which support the execution of the company's core competencies, should serve the focal company in acquiring new skills, competencies, and knowledge.[3]

Prior to diving into the criteria for considering make-or-buy decisions, it is worth noting one further type of a supplier relationship. Consider the continuum that was discussed earlier, with tactical decisions on one end and strategic on the other. Further along the strategic continuum is an option termed "strategic alliances." These types of relationships require the highest level of trust and collaboration since each party to the alliance typically provides knowledge and expertise. While risk-sharing is a benefit to these arrangements, alliances contain the highest level of risk as strategic and operational information is shared within the alliance. While most companies explore or maintain alliances with other companies, these are not discussed in this book.

This is because they necessitate a slightly different and deeper analysis than is required by make-or-buy decisions.

Considerations and Criteria for Make-or-Buy Project Decisions

The process starts with revisiting the core fundamentals discussed in Part 1 of the book: who is the company and what do they do? Current company strategy provides direction on what the company should be concentrating on. Further, the business strategy for operations (operations is used broadly to include any operations, manufacturing, or other team, generating revenue for the company) will help identify where the core competencies reside. A make-or-buy decision needs to be aligned with the business strategy.

In conjunction with corporate and business strategy, there must be a clear understanding of how the company creates value. Further, how effective is the company at creating value? This requires a tangible way to measure, such as benchmarking against other companies in the industry. Key indicators can provide evidence as to whether the focal company is effective at creating value. My experience has been that many companies are not well-versed at developing a strategy nor at understanding how they create value.

In vertically integrated companies, attempting to quantify the value creation for each of the operating groups, along with understanding the collective value of the combined operating groups, is not well understood. How the company is organized (e.g., an organizational chart with reporting structures) along with an understanding of the company culture also play a role in determining value. Determining value at the company is a complex issue and not explored in this book.

To conduct the make-or-buy decision, the operations, accounting, or supply chain team will conduct a financial analysis. Your role as a supply chain professional will be to conduct a full analysis of all the relevant factors and incorporate the financial analysis into your work. Next, you will work with both internal stakeholders and suppliers to make decisions and recommendations.

Aside from RBV, decision making criteria can be quite varied; consider each of the items on the list below in relation to your company as they relate to primary activities to create value. Analyze relevant criteria on the list to determine the impact both short term and long term. Once individually analyzed, a list of relevant criteria should be developed. The items on the list should be considered together to determine the overall impact on the business.

Services Versus Goods

Although the decision making process is relatively similar, the ability to evaluate make-or-buy decisions with a service requires unique criteria. Services are explored within their own chapter in this book.

Proprietary Products

Consider any recipes, manufacturing, or assembly process, patents, or patents-pending for confidentiality. For example, many fast-food products are made in a central location and then distributed to various retail locations. This approach suggests that the key strength of the retail sites resides in selling the product and maintaining the facility versus baking the products. The approach also keeps proprietary information in one centralized location. Consider who has access to the product information.

Capital Investment

Consider the example discussed above with proprietary products. Having a centralized facility make the products requires one single investment. Requiring each retail facility to make and bake their own products requires both space and an investment in various kitchen equipment, which can be costly. In other situations, consider the cost to upgrade or replace equipment, particularly if a technology upgrade is a part of the investment. It may be more effective to outsource the manufacturing and avoid the capital cost. The finance (or accounting) team can weigh in on the criteria to understand the financial gain of keeping in-house. Operations will need to evaluate how strategic the manufacturing process is to the business and the risk of moving this outside the company.

Union

Any operation which is unionized may require external expertise to interpret local laws regarding the impact of closing a facility, operations, and outsourcing the activity. Consider the publicity and potential impact to the company's reputation surrounding such a move. Evaluate the same criteria if considering a make decision.

Market Competitiveness

Determine the key attributes of how the company competes in the market; does the company do something specialized or different which brings a competitive edge? For example, does the company provide a level of experience difficult to find in the market that customers are willing to pay for? Is the company more flexible, with a high level of quality or brand recognition not found with suppliers?

Supplier Issues

Analyze the supplier landscape with key issues such as lead time required, distribution coverage, a competent supplier or, conversely, a supplier that has specialized know-how, volume required that is too little for the company or too little for a supplier, warehouse or transportation issues and costs, multiple-supplier strategy, or the risk of a supply chain disruption.

Product Maturity and Lifecycle

Newer products or services tend to be more proprietary versus products that are near the end of their lifecycle. Consider the capital investment required for older products with declining sales and determine if it is still a worthwhile investment.

Data and Information Security

Determine whether your data could be considered proprietary and at risk. General sales of products similar to those at other companies is important information but may not be considered proprietary. For example, how much soda one grocery store sells versus another is likely similar, and profit margins as a category will be similar. Determine the impact of any leaked information and whether this information should be in the hands of an outsourced company.

Economies of Scale (EOS)

This applies to both developing EOS within the company or outsourcing with an EOS supplier. EOS can provide lower expenses and higher quality. Consider the following with EOS: incremental expenses with labor and materials, inventory and warehouse holding, manufacturing, and operations. With the fuel delivery example, there were no economies of scale with sites spread out across a large geography. In addition, this was a mid-size company. Therefore, it was logical to hand this activity off to a company which could provide an EOS with their large operations.

Morale

Make-or-buy decisions can impact the morale of the people currently doing the work. In addition, it can impact the level of trust between leadership and employees by outsourcing an activity. Similarly, bringing the activity in-house can have a positive impact. Consider the impact not only to operations but also on morale, which can impact colleagues in other functions too.

Cost Savings

Although the decision should never be made solely on cost, cost is a key factor to consider. Recall the discussion on outsourcing the fuel delivery; in this scenario, there are still costs if this activity is to be fully outsourced since someone needs to manage contracts and service delivery. Cost is explored further in the decision making process.

PESTEL

PESTEL stands for political, economic, social, technological, environmental, or legal issues. Explore and analyze anything that could impact the operations today or over the next few years. A change in legislation could have a severe impact. For example, environmental laws focusing on manufacturing inputs, or the process, could require substantial changes and costs to the business.

Risk

A catch-all phrase means to think about anything that could impact the business. Seek out employees who have been through a similar experience or have been on the make-or-buy side for insight into the pros and cons. Risk is discussed in Chapter 5.

Ethics

Do you have visibility into your supplier's suppliers. Do you know enough about the company the team proposes to outsource the good or service to? Does that company align with the same values as your company? All of this should be known and considered before outsourcing. Do your research on both the proposed supply company along with their suppliers. Get to know their operations - ensure their adherence to laws (e.g., safety, human rights, and whether they pay bribes) is like your own - and that they are not breaking laws, locally and where they conduct business operations.

Automation

A substitute for making a good or service in-house is automating the process. Consider this possibility in conjunction with the capital expenditure option along with current expenses for operating the business. Involve the finance team in a cost-benefit analysis of a capital spend versus the operations expenditure. Also consider the impact of changing something that the company is known for. For example, if quality is an attribute, evaluate whether automating could be positively or negatively impacted..

Strategic Alliance

Due to the uniqueness and range of possibilities of alliances, supply chain professionals can consider other forms of make-or-buy decisions and whether the goal can be achieved in a unique arrangement and through a mutually beneficial relationship.

Summary

The list provided is certainly not exhaustive, and readers should consider other criteria that might be unique to a particular industry or product and service. Regardless of the arrangement, always consider the question "what is at risk?" (refer to Chapter 5—Risk). Ensure both opportunities and negative impacts are considered and analyzed.

Make-or-Buy Decision Making Project Process

Perhaps the first and most important piece of information to know when conducting a make-or-buy decision is that these are typically highly sensitive decisions and, therefore, can be emotionally charged. This is because the outcome of a decision might include shutting down a segment of the business, which could require a layoff of employees. Layoffs impact employee livelihood, morale, and families. They sometimes impact entire communities and may bring unwanted but warranted media attention. For example, suppose a company operates a plant in a small community that happens to be the main employer. The shutdown will not only impact employees but also can extend to other businesses as well, such as local suppliers and the hospitality industry. Treat these decisions with respect and be aware of the possible domino effect while ensuring that your company has the necessary tools and support processes in place. Of course, the reverse is also true; there is nothing more exciting than having a new major employer move in and create jobs, opportunities, and taxes for the community.

The external community may not have a choice as to which companies come and go or expand. However, within the company, employees will generally have a voice in major decisions and, therefore, these can become emotionally charged and politically motivated. Senior leaders want to protect their teams from shutdowns or, conversely, have new opportunities fall within their portfolio. Therefore, an ideal first step is to recruit a neutral person to conduct the review, such as an external consultant or consulting company that is well versed in conducting make-or-buy decisions. A consultant will help keep personal interests out of the decision and instead keep everyone aligned on the decision making criteria and process.

Phase 1: Project Definition

To arrive at this phase, it should be clear why the company is pursuing this project. Therefore, the first step will be to outline the goal(s) of the endeavor. Again, the goal should never be solely on cost. There must be other instigating factors. For example, is the company trying to become more competitive with, or diversify, their products? Has the competitive landscape changed in recent years—either with inputs (e.g., suppliers) or involving outputs (e.g., customers, competitors, and regulatory)? Does nearshoring or offshoring make more sense than it did in the past? Determining how the company plans to create or maintain value in the market should be the primary factor. The goal should clearly demonstrate how the business would create new or additional value, and how it would be aligned to the strategy and objectives.

Further defining the project occurs in the first phase. A leader will need to sanction the project, which is essentially granting permission for the project to be explored. The size and dollar value of the project will determine what level of leader will need to sanction the project. The leader is typically titled the "project sponsor."

The sponsor will assign a project manager to lead the project. Depending on the size and sensitivity of the project, this could be an external consultant or a supply chain employee. It might also be an employee or group within the company that represents the function where the project has been initiated. The project team may consist of just the project manager or, depending on the size and opportunity of the project, it could be a large team, representing different functions from throughout the company.

Writing a charter at this stage of the project is required. The charter contains important information about the project manager, the sponsor, and the key stakeholders, such as a steering team. Key stakeholders should include those who will be authorized to weigh in on a decision. Other stakeholders who could provide critical information or could disrupt the project, such as suppliers, customers, or the outside community, should also be included (and listed in your risk registry). The goal statement should be added to the charter. Next is determining how the decision will be measured and what to include as success factors. Risks associated with the make-or-buy decision should be documented in the charter. Finally, the charter includes the statement of work (SOW). The SOW includes the scope of work, deliverables, and timelines, and any other relevant information. This document serves as a formal agreement between the project manager and the sponsor.

The scope of the work to be completed in the project should clearly outline what the project is to achieve. For example, are all the plants underperforming or just one? In these early stages, does the project initiator or the project team have enough information about what part of the plant(s) is underperforming in regard to people, processes, or outdated technology? And why? The ability to be specific is very important to capture so that a thorough analysis can be completed. If the team is unsure, then this is information to be explored further. Finally, the scope of work should outline what is out of scope. For example, any plants or geography that might not be impacted could be out of scope.

If the company has formal project processes, then these should be included and followed to ensure all company requirements are addressed in the make-or-buy decision project.

Phase 2: Information Gathering

The second phase is the information-gathering phase of the project. Seek out data and information that support the project goals and provide a basis for a value-creating decision. The list of data and information must align to the scope developed in Phase 1; however, the people should be open.

Gather information supporting the core competencies of the company. Industry information is required to assess and support whether the company has a competitive advantage and, if so, quantify how. For example, industry benchmarking information or trade association information can provide a basis for comparison. Accounting financial ratios are another. Any ethically sourced information on competitors is also helpful. For example, asking the sales team to provide information about the competitive landscape. Suppliers can provide general information about the marketplace, sharing what they can about their own strategy or about upcoming changes they might be making or trends they are seeing in the marketplace. These are all examples of ethically sourced information. Never ask a supplier to provide confidential information about a competitor. Not only is this unethical, but you can guarantee they will not hesitate to share your company's confidential information with your competitors!

Here is one other note on assessing the core competencies of your company. This is where an outside consultant or having the supply chain function lead a make-or-buy decision can provide value. It is common for a functional leader to protect their people and assets by not fairly assessing whether a function or a company truly has a competitive advantage in the marketplace. A neutral person has no stake in the outcome of the decision and can, therefore, look at the data or information through an unbiased lens and make a value-creating decision. The consultant or supply chain person will want to make sure that they fairly capture market nuances that only the people working in operations understand; however, there needs to be an unbiased review of the information.

Incorporate Criteria

Determine the evaluation criteria required to complete an analysis. Forming high-level evaluation questions aligned with the project goals and scope should help cut through what could be a lot of data while directing the work. The previous section outlined important considerations and criteria for making a make-or-buy decision. These need to be weighed and discussed to determine how they might contribute to a make-or-buy decision. The evaluation questions, along with the criteria chosen for the project, should be reviewed for thoroughness with the project sponsor and with any other key decision maker.

Risks

A risk registry should be established early in the project. It should outline all the possible and potential risks that may occur in the project. Each of these should be discussed on a regular basis by the project team (e.g., bi-weekly or monthly). Risks that are occurring should be managed on an ongoing basis and tracked.

Continuum of Supplier Relationship

Determine if the outsourcing concept is more tactical or strategic and why. Define scope and criticality.

Suppliers

Complete an analysis of the suppliers. First, if the company is to make the product, determine and evaluate the availability of suppliers to provide inputs as raw materials. Since these materials would be an input into a primary activity, an analysis must be completed. To assess the suppliers, include factors such as quality, reliability, geographical coverage, and pricing. Think outside the box. For example, if your company has no storage, they might need regular small shipments; can the supplier provide the lot size required? And because the company is considering outsourcing the activity, an analysis of the supplier(s) who would be making the product or conducting the service is also required. The project team needs to generate a list of criteria required for outsourcing the activity. Use caution when contacting suppliers, if at all, in this critical stage of the project.

Also note that supply chain efficiency should be examined (determine where value is lost or gained). Evaluate the suppliers providing the inputs into the transformation process. For example, if outsourcing the activity is being considered, but only one or two key producers exist, which are also making your competitor's products, determine if this is the best route for your company. Or, for example, any new suppliers; understand why and how this might help or hurt your industry, understand why and how this might help or hurt your industry. For example, I completed an evaluation on behalf of a local company to examine the possibility of importing refined product (gasoline and diesel) into a specific geography. While the product could be sourced more economically outside the local market, including transportation, the more important question was to consider the impact to the current supply and demand market. To import additional product would totally upset the existing equilibrium in the local market, causing prices to fall. The outcome? It would not make sense to import product. However, the value in the consulting project was realizing that local refined product prices were hyper-inflated, which provided a bargaining position for my client. This example serves to suggest the need to constantly be assessing the market for changes and new opportunities.

Phase 3: Analysis

All the raw data and information gathered to this point will be fully analyzed within this phase. The analysis will include both a make and a buy decision. Further, a "make" decision requires both an internal analysis and an external analysis be conducted. Likewise, with a "buy" decision. This process needs an unbiased and transparent approach in order to generate insights in which the project team can make a value-based decision.

While the make or buy risks were generated in the first two phases, in this phase, the associated risks will be further analyzed. These risks are separate from any project risks (e.g., project budget or sponsor risk) which are ongoing, recorded in the risk registry, and managed through-out the project.

A financial analysis needs to include both capital costs and operating costs. Suppose the goal is to evaluate building a new warehouse, the financial analysis would include the capital cost to build the new warehouse along with the additional costs to make the warehouse functional such as shelves, forklifts, furniture, and technology housed within. The operating costs would include any expense allocated for the ongoing operation, such as lease payments or taxes, labor, raw materials, utilities, and overhead.

Years ago, I did a small consulting project for a marketing company. They were looking at introducing a product to their service based company. Their costs included the cost to launch the new product. However, they failed to include other relevant costs. This would include costs associated with recruiting the new employee who would be selling the product, along with ongoing expenses for this new position (e.g., salary, bonus, medical and dental, and so on), their vehicle and insurance, desk and laptop, space in the building (a price per sq. foot), just to name a few. In addition to the employee costs, there could be warehouse and distribution costs for the product, ongoing marketing, and so on. While the list may feel endless, remember that if a company decides to go to market to buy the product from a supplier, that supplier's product costs would be passed on to your company along with their profit margin. The reason for making a make or buy decision should never be made on cost but rather on how the goals and strategy of the company are fulfilled while never neglecting the total cost of a change.

Another cost to evaluate is how the support activities are allocated in the company. In some companies, this carries the term "corporate overhead." Support activities include the key support activities in the value chain such as Human Resources, Technology, and Procurement. It also includes "firm infrastructure" which is a "catch-all" of the remaining functions of company infrastructure (i.e., legal, communications, environmental, and other functions which vary from company to company).

There are two distinguishing factors about the support activities. First, they are not involved in the day-to-day production of the company's goods and services. That does not suggest these functions are not vitally important to the company—in fact, the opposite. The company is a system and needs all functions, including the key support activities, to function as a viable system. Second, the support activities are not revenue-generating functions. Therefore, they are labeled as corporate overhead—they are a cost to the business. There are a variety of ways to allocate these costs. Some companies assign a percent of the total overhead cost, others embed the services into operations, and others use a fee per usage or some other arrangement. Be sure to work with the accounting function to understand how this cost is allocated and its impact on the company. Better yet, if you have profit and loss responsibility (i.e., P&L), you need to be intimately familiar with what is included in each line item on your reports.

A final question to consider in this phase is to determine how the company will scale up to become proficient or, alternatively, how they will divest and outsource the activity. Risks to operations and the company during this time period should also be included! For example, when a company decides to drop a supplier and instead produce a product internally, expect subpar service from the supplier during the transition period. The financial analysis will also include operating costs during the scaling-up period. For example, consider all recruitment and selection costs for the employees, the training program, and so on. These cannot be overlooked.

To conduct a "buy" decision, there are additional considerations to evaluate when the company is going to market with a product or service. First, consider the impact on the company to shut down and downsize the current operation. For example, which people will be impacted and how will this be resolved (e.g., transferred to another division), along with the cost to downsize or transfer. Consider what to do with the assets. Ideally, they would be transferred to another function within the company. Use caution with any assets to be sold into the public market as depending on what these are, evaluate whether it will potentially give a competitor a competitive advantage.

Determine any one-time costs. For example, if the operations are conducted on leased land, determine the buyout of the lease.

Next, with a buy decision, certain costs will remain with the company. Oversight activities may include contract negotiation and maintenance, overseeing product quality, organizing logistics, receiving products, and reviewing accounts payable, to name some of the more obvious activities. It is important to build and maintain a relationship with the supplier; this takes time and effort.

Finally, consider other factors which could impact the make or buy decision. Be sure to calculate intangible costs. For example, closing company operations located within a small community may severely impact the community, especially if the focal company is the main employer in town. In addition, negative publicity may further hurt the company name and reputation. Consider other intangible factors such as the culture of the two companies—are they compatible?

There is a myriad of issues to consider ranging from supplier location, length of time for product to arrive, or the spend with a supplier, to the criticality of the product or service to operations. Build a list which is relevant to your company operations and complete the required analysis. The bottom line is that if the company is being run with poor internal operations and fails to conduct a thorough make or buy decision, jumping to engage a new supplier could result in higher risk than the current situation.

Phase 4: Decision Making and Recommendation

This final phase in the project requires finalizing the decision and providing a recommendation to the decision maker (e.g., the project sponsor or steering team). Prior to submitting a recommendation, the project team will want to vet their initial findings with the decision maker for their initial reaction and test whether further evaluation is required. Remember, these are often emotionally and politically charged decisions, so pretesting initial thoughts may be more relevant in certain companies, or cultures, than in others.

The last step in this phase is to determine how the recommendation will be measured. This should be based on a couple of factors. First, a measurement that is aligned with the strategy and goals of the company; how will this action support these? Second, return to the reason the make or buy project was conducted—was the current operation uncompetitive? Was the company trying to expand into a new market? Whatever the reason(s), a means to measure would need to be laid out in the recommendation. There may also be intangible reasons such as employee or customer satisfaction.

Following the recommendation, this phase of the project may be complete or the decision maker may require the project team to develop an action plan for next steps. If no further work is required, the project team would move to Phase 5—project closure.

Phase 5: Project Closure

Following the recommendation to the decision maker, the project team will prepare for the project team to disband. A few key activities should occur prior to this step.

The project team will conduct a "lessons learned," containing what went well and what could have been done better. Next, revisit and close the risk registry. Close off any correspondence with suppliers, key stakeholders, or experts involved in the process, such as consultants or lawyers. If there was a project team, the resources committed to the project will be disbanded along with other resources and returned to the function leaders and resource owners.

There may be a handoff to an implementation team who will execute the recommendations from the project team.

Finally, prepare a final report and retain it as an artifact for future discovery. It should include the reason(s) for the project and who initiated it. Ensure information reflective of the current market conditions is captured. This might include market economics, company RBV, supplier landscape, available products, and services.

Outline the project process the team followed. Include the project findings and how and why the team arrived at their recommendation. Next, provide the decision from the key decision makers along with the reason for their decision.

Last, provide the team's lessons learned. Discuss any issues encountered along the journey and recommendations to improve the process. Be sure to include any key artifacts such as supplier proposals and e-mails, key stakeholder issues, surveys, or anything else that the team used as key decision making points.

Measure and Governance

Following the completion of Phase 5, the project team has been disbanded and the company has operationalized the work of the project. The next step is to determine whether a value-creating decision was made and, if so, what were the contributing factors and the results of the decision.

The following are suggestions for contracting with suppliers which provide a means of both governance and measurement.

Establish your own service agreements rather than using your suppliers'. This allows your company to set a standard and incorporate your company needs. Then when sourcing suppliers, provide a problem statement laying out the business need as opposed to stating that you need "A, B, and C;" you may receive some very creative results which you had not considered. It also opens the door for fruitful negotiations and establishment of relationship governance. This creativity can be worked into contracts and may provide an opportunity for innovation. Consider all incentives for innovation (along with penalties for failure to perform).

For make decisions, your company will require time to ramp up to full capability. This should have been included within the project phases and outlined for the operations team who will have responsibility for managing the implementation. Include how the decision will be measured during this time period. This is a critical step which requires monitoring because the failure to achieve targets can cause risks across the value chain. Therefore, any deviations from the plan should be discovered, understood, and corrected.

For an outsource (buy) decision, the work can be far more rigorous and involved than anticipated. Outsourcing can also hold far more risk than a make decision. As both companies begin working together, the differences in company culture and how work is performed at each company will begin to surface. This can impact the relationship and the anticipated results. Any company requirements which were not built into the contract may be difficult to enforce. To prevent this, open and effective dialog and negotiations between the two parties are vital to establishing a positive and fruitful relationship. Capture this and build it into contracts. Both parties may wish to engage with legal representation during the contracting process. Keep in mind a "perfect" contract may still result in poor performance by either party. It can take years to enforce the contract through the court system while incurring significant legal fees and further damaging a delicate relationship. Once relationships have turned sour, it is highly likely the operations of both companies are impacted. Therefore, regardless of the contract status, effective contract management occurs in the day-to-day relationship of both the operations team and the supply chain functions in both companies.

Researchers surveyed executives to understand more about their outsourcing relationship and uncovered some insightful and interesting results.[5] First, a key finding was that most leaders had underestimated the time required to successfully build and manage the relationship with an outsourced supplier. They realized there was a surprising amount of time and challenges involved. Outsourcing decisions cannot be handed off to a supplier with an expectation of success.

A second key finding from the survey was that only half of the leaders were satisfied with their outsourcing relationship.[5] Many found it difficult to manage the supplier relationship, particularly with strategic outsourcing decisions. The strategy, goals, culture, and priorities of one company can be very different from their partner's and will be uncovered quickly. The process the two parties use to work through and manage these differences is critical in the early stages of the relationship. Ignoring them will usually make the differences worse. Managing them can be accomplished through dedicated time for open and transparent communication. Enlisting the expertise of an experienced change management consultant (or similar) can help facilitate joint problem-solving sessions and a process for working constructively together.

In a similar study, the researchers found a key success factor to any partnership was the willingness of members to collaborate and problem-solve jointly.[6] Bidirectional and open information sharing was considered to be a key success factor. What contributed to this list was the willingness to build mutual trust along with the quality of communication and participation in the relationship. Therefore, careful consideration, up front, of the time involved in managing the relationship should be discussed and the governance process laid out. Members should be willing to devote additional resources to the relationship to support the mutual success of each party.

Summary

Make or buy project decisions are an important step for any company to consider, as markets evolve and change, and these decisions should always be in play and monitored. That is, what doesn't make sense to outsource today might make sense with changing market conditions tomorrow. These projects can be emotionally charged, which can have an impact not only on employees within the company but can extend to the community within which a company operates.

While cost is a determining factor, it should never be the primary one. First and foremost, the project goals should be aligned with the strategy and goals of the company. For make or buy decisions, a project process was outlined which includes decision-making criteria. These decisions vary by scope and criticality of the what is being outsourced. Scope and criticality are closely aligned with the primary activities of Porter's value chain. Tactical decisions can be made relatively easier, while strategic decisions require far greater scrutiny.

Outsourcing decisions are not meant to "make a problem go away," as outsourced work requires substantial relationship-building and ongoing work with a supplier to ensure that the goals of both parties are achieved. Further, these relationships can result in lost productivity and damaged reputations with customers and other suppliers. However, supplier relationships that are chosen carefully, have a well-thought-out contract, and are managed effectively can be a source of innovation and competitive advantage.

Application Questions

1. Discuss three pros of plural sourcing. Discuss three cons.
2. Explain how Porter's value chain should inform make or buy project decisions.
3. Provide a strategic example of outsourcing and discuss three ways you can ensure the relationship is successful.

Project Case Scenario

During my time working with a large refiner and marketing company, I was responsible for many retail assets. My company had formed a joint venture with a large international retailer a few years prior. The venture consisted of that retailer subleasing land at each of their large box stores to our company. Our company built small kiosks for confectionary sales in addition to selling fuel products. Keeping with the strategy of the large retailer, our business was positioned to be hyper-competitive with our pricing. While our sites grew to have a strong brand presence, it was apparent that this new business stream would never be profitable. To be successful in the retail fuel industry, a site must either sell a significant volume or there must be ancillary income such as a convenience store or car wash.

My first responsibility as an employee is to ensure the business is viable and profitable and second, to look for value-creating opportunities to further increase the value of a business. I soon realized this line of business would never be viable. I shared my concerns with my senior leader.

The senior leader formed a small project team to evaluate options. We examined numerous opportunities, such as shortening the operating hours or turning the sites into unattended ones with no staff present. Alternatively, the team evaluated the cost of shutting down the sites and cutting our losses. Finally, we looked at other unique options such as subleasing the small kiosks to other industry entrepreneurs, such as mini drive-through coffee shops, or to a dry-cleaning chain that might be interested in taking over the network.

Questions

1. Determine why this is a make or buy project decision.
2. Discuss the opportunities the team put forward. Generate other alternatives.
3. Discuss why the decision to speak to the leader was a value-creating decision.
4. Assume the subleasing arrangement made sense; determine if the project choice is strategic or tactical.

CHAPTER 7

Service-Based Project Decisions

Learning Objectives

- Explain why the production of services is so difficult to manage compared to the production of goods.
- Use criteria to differentiate a good compared to a service.
- Discuss goods compared to services as they relate to the value chain.
- Discuss the importance of having a service strategy.
- Discuss standardization and how it can support service delivery.

Introduction

Suppose you have been asked to source and evaluate consultants that will provide safety training for your function. What is the process you would follow to evaluate the companies? You might start by looking on the Internet and googling "safety training." After reviewing the material on websites, you narrow the search to two companies. Prior to contacting them, let's step back and review your initial plan. Did you look for specific credentials associated with a company? Did you uncover reviews to read and evaluate what customers have stated about the providers? What criteria did you use to evaluate which company is more qualified or better suited for your company and business needs?

I always chuckle when I am driving down the highway and see a sign at a road-stop restaurant that states something like "world's best pie!" Does that little place on the side of the highway truly have the world's best pies? Will they have an award on the wall when you walk inside? Likely not. Once you start eating the pie, you will judge whether the pie is excellent or not. Many companies will market themselves as best in class and state that they are better than their competitors. Evaluating a good is much easier; perhaps, the pie could be the world's best. However, with a service, what criteria would you apply to the wait staff bringing you that piece of pie? A service is much more difficult to evaluate than a good and can be highly subjective. Often, time and experience with the service provider are required to make a fair evaluation. However, this step only occurs once a contract has been signed and the service is being provided. So, what criteria can be used to evaluate a service provider?

This book could have included deep information and guidance on inventory, quality, or distribution, but instead it includes services. The reasons why will be explored in this section, but the main reason is that evaluating a service is extremely difficult to do well. In fact, a survey suggests that 75 percent of respondents state it is difficult, or very difficult, to contract for a service versus a good.[1] And most companies which provide a service state that it is difficult to provide a consistent, repeatable, and efficient service for their customers. Finally, services are difficult to market and sell. Services are so difficult for researchers to study that even the academic community seems to shy away from this topic given the limited research. That said, some excellent research does exist which will be explored in this chapter.

The intangible nature of services makes it difficult for purchasers of a service to quantify and clarify expectations in supply chain agreements. Supply chain professionals who can be effectively granular with their service contracts can create value and reduce risk for their company. In fact, this is a highly sought-after skill for companies. This capability can be rewarded with the potential for 40 percent higher compensation associated with contracting for a good.[2]

Strategic Differences Between Goods and Services

It is important to understand just how important services are by looking at what is produced globally. The standard measure of value created by the production of goods and services in a country is their Gross Domestic Product (GDP).[3] Of all the goods and services produced, services make up the largest percentage of the total global GDP at 65 percent.[4] That figure has remained relatively constant over the past 30 years. Services represent more than 70 percent of everything produced in most Western countries. In Canada, services as a total of everything produced have grown from 63 percent in 1995 to 67 percent in present day. In the United States, over the same time period, that number is even higher, growing from 72 to 78 percent.

Consider the wide variety of services that exist. They include those provided by professionals such as lawyers, accountants, and consultants. Professional services are also delivered by the healthcare industry by doctors, nurses, and a variety of specialists, such as cardiologists, and in related industries by physiotherapists, massage therapists, chiropractors, social workers, and other professions. Many others are based on skilled trades such as lawn care, hair salons, and dry cleaning. Services are critical to any developed, division-of-labor economy.

Services can be categorized as follows: wholesale and retail, finance and insurance, real estate, health care, professional and technical services, personal services, education, hotels and restaurants, culture and recreation, transportation and warehouse, utilities, and government services.[5]

There are many definitions of what a "service supply chain" is; this definition captures the essence and complexity of what it means to compete as a service-based company and what it means for a supplier or customer to contract with a service-based company:

> Intangible, labour intensive, heterogeneous, it cannot be stored and transported because production and consumption occur simultaneously, have a high level of customer influence, and have a quality dimension that often is difficult to judge.[6]

This definition makes it clear that the process can be rather complex. Thus, a company producing a good rather than providing a service requires a different approach to managing the delivery of the service. A good suggests that there is a tangible output, such as a pencil or a vehicle. A material item that can be seen, touched, or felt is ready for sale and can be delivered. This criterion indicates that ownership transfer can be determined between seller and buyer. Contrast this with a service. A service implies an act—someone has done something for us. This makes it difficult, if not impossible, to determine when ownership transfers (i.e., when is the haircut yours?). This is in part because a service lacks a physical identity. In essence, a service cannot be owned but can be used and, therefore, cannot be returned. Typically, the point of sale serves as the basis for consumption of services.

Measuring the value received from a service can be complicated and may be affected by individual preference. How can one evaluate a service and then determine whether a contract was fulfilled? This is the difficulty of service-based projects.

Every company resides on a continuum where, at one end, the company exists to provide goods, such as a clothing store. Or, at the other end of the continuum, a company may be a pure service, such as an accounting firm. Most companies, however, are a hybrid of a good and a service. For example, most car dealerships also offer vehicle repair and maintenance. Or, as a service company, a hair salon or spa sells beauty products such as shampoos and lotions. Globally, employment in services has been steadily increasing to 51 percent in 2019 versus 34 percent in 1991.[4] In both Canada and the United States, that number has increased from 71 to 79 percent.[4] Because of this trend, employing knowledge workers has become an essential requirement as services remain the most rapidly growing sector.[4]

There are six criteria used to evaluate how a good differs from a service. First is the uniformity of input. Consider a good such as a t-shirt. The manufacturing plant must start the production process with the same inputs each time so that the output is consistently the same. For example, sourcing and procuring the same cotton from the same suppliers with specific quality standards. With a service, no two service providers will have the same job experience, training, education, or creative approach; the uniformity of input will differ. There may be uniformity with the tools the provider uses, such as the scissors with hair stylists.

Second is the measure of productivity. Productivity measures how productive or efficient a company is at turning their inputs into outputs. It is an important measure of wealth in an economy. Productivity can be further broken down to evaluate where opportunities to become more productive may reside, or where a company excels at what they do. For example, how many widgets a machine can produce per hour or how much energy a machine uses to produce those widgets are both important measures of a company's productivity.

It is much easier to measure productivity with a good—such as how many t-shirts are manufactured per hour. With a service, comparing the work of two hair stylists is difficult. Often, a stylist will work on two clients at the same time—hair color is applied on one client and then while that client waits 45 minutes for the color to set, the stylist will be cutting another client's hair. In addition, the number of customers might be tracked per day, but how long each stylist takes with each customer is not something typically tracked by a company. Some stylists might have an assistant who helps with washing a client's hair and prepping them, while the stylist is busy cutting another client's hair. Therefore, it is difficult and time-consuming to track meaningful productivity.

There is a link between productivity and profitability. Individual companies should seek a means to measure their labor productivity and determine whether that number is increasing or decreasing. Most companies can obtain industry information with benchmark data that provides key indicators. It can be arduous to measure productivity, but very useful for benchmarking in order to improve operations, create value, and, ultimately, profitability. For these reasons, services are more difficult to manage, but not impossible.

Third is the uniformity of output. Consider our example of the hair stylist. No two customers have the same hair (inputs). However, assume two customers both want the exact same haircut and explain this goal to two hairstylists. Based on the stylists' experience and understanding of the customers' request, it is likely that the two customers will not get the exact same haircut. In addition, the time it takes to cut and style the hair will vary between the two stylists. The complexities related to the inputs, productivity level, and outputs make it very difficult to find an easy method of comparing and measuring two stylists at the same salon.

Fourth, quality. Recall the Project Management Institute's definition of quality management from Chapter 2: "the degree to which a set of inherent characteristics fulfills requirements."[7] Because quality is an abstract concept associated with price and longevity, evaluating quality with a good is far easier than with a service. While a worker can spot a defect in a good, it is much more difficult to do in a service and can be very subjective. Therefore, how do we define a "good" consultant or a "good" delivery driver?

When making value-creating project decisions, it is very important that quality is defined. The definition outlines what the level of service is to the customer (what's included) and must be consistently provided every single time (quality assurance). For example, offering customers a cup of coffee or tea before they meet with the consultant or hairstylist is a quality statement and helps define the service to be provided. Forgetting to offer this will impact the customer experience and the level of quality expected by customers. Note that for this to be a value-creating decision, there must be value created with the "free" cup of coffee, such as repeat customer business. If it only serves to cost the company money with no defined benefit, it is not likely a value-creating decision.

Fifth is customer contact. Goods can be produced with no customer contact. A service is performed and, therefore, requires personal contact between provider and customer. Depending on the service, it may require a high level of customer contact so that the request can be shared with the service provider. In addition, because a service is an act provided, the final output and quality level in part is determined by the level of communication during the process of providing the service. Service supply chains can involve multiple people and suppliers in the service creation and delivery phase.[8]

Last is final output. A good is tangible, a service is intangible. It is very easy to compare, count, and assess the quality of the final output for a good. It is much harder to do so for a service. For example, is the customer dissatisfied with their haircut because of the stylist or because the customer was unable to articulate what they wanted? Did the project fail (yes, a project is considered to be a service!) because it was a bad idea or the project manager was not experienced? Is the customer able to evaluate a poorly trained versus an experienced provider? There are many situations where the service provider has valuable knowledge that the customer may not be familiar with, which makes it difficult to ascertain the capability of the provider. For example, most people do not know much about computer programing and, therefore, must rely on the advice and suggestions of experts. How do we know when we should take a provider's advice and that we may regret it if we do not? It is difficult to assess whether a lawyer or accountant provides better service than the next. In summary, it can be difficult to make service-based decisions with certainty due to variations of the inputs, outputs, and quality.

In addition to the differences between goods and services, there are other important challenges in how services are managed. This includes supply chain issues of capacity and inventory. Capacity is the maximum output a company can produce in a specific time period. Capacity planning with a good is much easier. There may be peaks and valleys as a result of slow versus busy sales periods, but these will usually have a stable pattern. For example, gasoline sales for vehicles peak during the summer when people are traveling, or around important holidays. The demand for gardening tools, bedding plants, and flowers will peak in spring, and there will be little or no demand in winter. Producing goods at capacity enables the opportunity to store inventory. As the demand for a good fluctuates high or low, inventory can smooth out the differences. An unexpected rain storm at the beach will impact ice cream sales for the day. While the sales for ice cream that day will be low, the salesperson can save the inventory for the next day. This presents the second challenge of capacity for a service; the inability to store inventory. The service provider is the inventory. Without the provider, there is no service as a service cannot be stored for future use. Further, to satisfy higher demand with a service, it would require sourcing and securing additional service providers.

Capacity planning includes determining the optimal resources for producing a good or a service. This includes the tools and assets to produce the good or service, along with resources such as labor. Capacity is generally associated with both goods and services. For instance, a manufacturing plant can produce a certain number of widgets per day, and a massage therapist can book a client per hour, for a total of eight per day.

Knowing high-demand periods can be managed differently between goods and services. Extra shifts at the manufacturing plant can be added or products can be outsourced to a company having extra capacity, and where inventory can be stored for those peak time periods. With a service company, inventory cannot be stored but must occur at the time of service. This makes it much more difficult to plan capacity, and it can be more costly if a company gets the planning process wrong. In addition, the time it takes for the service provider to complete the service can be altered from plan. If a massage therapist's client is late or cancels at the last minute, the therapist's capacity (and profit) is impacted. With a doctor, the service can be faster than expected or take longer due to customers (patients) requesting changes or if there are complications with the service. Customer influence can have a significant impact on the service occurring in that moment or after the service has been completed, with issues such as customers requesting referrals, complaints, and follow-up issues needing resolution.

Due to the vast differences that exist between producing a good or a service, including capacity and inventory issues, it is more difficult to forecast, with certainty, business issues such as sales and profitability that arise with a service.

The final difference with respect to the topic of capacity pertains to location. A good can be manufactured anywhere in the world and be transported to the customer. A service must be conducted in proximity to the customer.

Goods and Services as They Relate to the Value Chain

Now that the key differences between goods and services have been laid out, it is a good time to discuss these as they relate to Porter's value chain. Recall from Chapter 2 that the value chain includes all the resources and processes required to produce and sell a product or service. The five primary activities in the value chain lay out where the value is created in a company. How effectively and efficiently these activities are executed will, in part, determine the costs and the ability of the company to generate a profit. All the primary activities are present with both a good and a service. However, there are variations between the two in how the activities are executed to create value, and these are outlined next.

The first difference is that with a good, the primary activities generally occur in a linear process. With a service, these activities may move back and forth during the service being performed. For example, during a landscaping contract, a customer may request additional trees and shrubs be added, which requires the landscaper to work with suppliers and plan the delivery. This requires a change in a project contract called a "change order" to adjust the scope, schedule, risk, and cost of the project. Because of variations that may occur when a service is being performed, it may be necessary for the service provider to maintain a variety of tools and inventory to use in fulfilling unexpected or unique requirements from customers.

Since a customer receives a service as it is being performed, the value chain outbound logistics takes on a different meaning. A service cannot be warehoused like a good can be, as the production and consumption of services occurs simultaneously. Finally, for marketing and sales, the service provider has an opportunity to add additional value during the service delivery. For example, while the landscaper is performing a service, they might also offer to sell tools to the customer that were used during the landscaping service; a hairstylist might recommend a shampoo or other hair styling products to their customer. The service provider may also seek feedback or ask for a formal review of the service that can serve as testimonials for future customers. After-sales support in both a good and a service helps with loyalty and customer retention.

Within the value chain, the support activities also have a role in aiding how service is delivered; however, only two of these will be addressed: human resource management and procurement. While human resource management is important to both creating a good and providing a service, it is vital for fulfilling a service. With a good, customers place more emphasis on the quality and features of the product, while also considering the sales and service received. With a service, having a knowledgeable, customer-focused, experienced service provider is a critical factor in the customer's overall satisfaction with the service. Human resource management focuses on attracting and recruiting valuable employees and programs aimed at training and retaining the provider.

Next, procuring goods and services (note: acquiring goods is called "procurement" or "purchasing," but for a service, the term is "service contracting"). Service contracting supports the service providers' ability to deliver a service and ultimately impacts the overall experience the customer receives. This requires a unique approach and process. The next section reviews the processes specific to managing a service.

Service Processes—Project Criteria for Value-Creating Decisions

Because a service is performed in conjunction with the customer, the primary activities do not occur in a linear process. Therefore, applying Porter's value chain to a good rather than a service must take a slightly different approach to create value. To support this, researchers have developed processes specific to services.[9] These demonstrate how a service supply chain interfaces and cuts across the primary activities. The processes also integrate and interface with suppliers and customers to deliver value. There are nine unique processes to help us to visualize how and when value is added within the primary activities.

The first process is service delivery management.[9] Perhaps most important, this service process articulates how a company establishes itself to fulfill their customer's needs. It includes how a company defines an order (size, frequency, and so on), creates the order, delivers the order, and enables and manages the value chain network to fulfill the promise. For example, consider the process of undergoing a surgery at a hospital. Patients start at admittance, where personal information and other information such as medical insurance are validated. Next, the patient moves to the surgical function, where a nurse receives the patient, asks them to change into a gown, checks vitals, discusses the process, places an IV, and so on. This is a simplified overview of a hospital's service delivery model. In this simplification, it would include all activities up until the patient is released and may even include a follow-up call from a doctor, or a representative, 24 hours after release.

Documenting this process is an important step for many reasons. For example, having a process assigns accountability and responsibility and ensures all members involved in providing the service know their role. It also helps define when one function is finished and when the next function begins (inputs and outputs). This is the means for achieving the work. Examining a process for efficiency and effectiveness is important. Business processes help a company determine where in the process value is created. Therefore, they provide a means for improving or increasing value. And finally, this can be used for training new employees and performance management.

The service delivery process can be evaluated by the customer. Therefore, there needs to be a means to measure the effectiveness of the service. For example, if 24-hour delivery is a commitment to customers as part of the service delivery, this can be measured. A word of caution: carefully monitor scope creep.[9] Scope creep is defined as a company consistently going above and beyond the requirements of the service delivery. This costs the company time and money (unless the business can demonstrate some sort of measurement such as an increase in sales and no loss in gross margin). Over time, it can become an expectation with buyers and, therefore, must be included in the service delivery.

The second process is customer relationship management (CRM). It requires building a clear and solid understanding of customers' needs along with the ability to meet those needs with the company's services (and goods). Engaging with customers on an ongoing basis is required in order to build knowledge for the purpose of sales. Engagement can occur in numerous ways, such as surveys, special offers, blogs and online communication, or customer appreciation events. Tracking and storing information about customers resides within the seventh process: information flow, defined below.

Measuring CRM entails an ability to track customer sales, determine profit, and identify which customers provide the most value to the company. For example, a business owner was concerned with the size of their database (3000 customers) and costs associated with data storage.

After analyzing the data, it was uncovered that most of their customers had made one-time purchases, and many had not purchased from the company in years. It became obvious that the business was paying to store information where most of it provided little or no economic value to the company. A value-creating decision would be to offload the non-value-add customers (to reduce data storage costs) and then analyze the cost/benefit of the shortened customer list to determine profitability versus time spent making those sales. Depending on the cost per customer, ongoing correspondence should be part of the marketing plan; however, a different level of engagement should occur with the shortened, preferred customer list. The more you know about your preferred customers, the more you can provide programs and services to support their needs and continue to validate the effectiveness of the service delivery model.

Third, supplier relationship management (SRM). Like CRM for service-based companies, it is recommended that the target company develop and maintain supplier relationships and view these as long-term partners. Recall that goods typically progress in a linear fashion (e.g., manufacturing to wholesale to retail), and services are produced and consumed simultaneously. Therefore, service delivery models are not linear but can and do shift back and forth. Having strong supplier relationships where the focal company is supported by supplier programs will help the company ensure service delivery. For example, a colleague rented a vehicle from a car rental company. They soon realized the vehicle was missing the windshield wiper blade and contacted the rental company. The rental company stated that they had an ongoing agreement with a well-known tire and muffler shop (which happens to have a location in almost every town and city). The colleague immediately drove the vehicle to the rental car's supplier, and the wiper blade was added in less than 5 minutes. While it was slightly inconvenient for the colleague to have to complete this activity, it was indeed a fantastic remedy compared to having to source a provider or to drive the car back to the rental car company. This provides insight into how a supplier can help ensure their customer (the car rental company) can effectively deliver their service model to customers.

To measure SRM, the service provider must have a clear understanding of their own needs as a business and be able to express this in the scope of work in their RFP.[9] The contract must reflect the SOW and service level required. For example, the supplier and service provider might determine the delivery frequency for goods or it could include a supplier-response time. It is not uncommon for agreements with trades (electrician and plumber) to respond to service calls and be on-site within a specified time. Numerous other measurements can be developed, such as delivery performance, lead time versus industry norm, supplier pricing versus the market, supply booking procedures, among others.[10] Note that the more demands are placed upon the supplier, the more risk the supplier will incur, which may be reflected in price and the ability to find a supplier willing to work with your company. Within Chapter 4, strategy and goals were discussed. Consider what drives your company's success and work with suppliers to support your company's ability to fulfill these (your company cannot be everything to everyone and still be competitive). Ensure the statement of work places the priorities aimed at driving value in your company. For example, Starbucks coffee competes on variety, quality, and consistency and not on speed or the lowest price. Build these criteria into supplier relationships.

Fourth, cash flow management. The cash-to-cash cycle is an important process for a company to understand because it traces the cash flow from raw material supply purchases until cash is collected from customers.[11] This includes facilitating the flow (how payments will be made) and the timing of payments across the supply chain, which includes your customers (buyers) and suppliers and may include transfer payments within a company. This is an important measurement as the timing can have an impact on the company, suppliers, customers, and profitability.

Fifth, demand management defined as the process which balances the customers' requirements with the firm's supply capabilities.[12] It is the company's ability to match supply with demand. Recall that a service cannot hold inventory to match peaks and valleys. However, finding the right balance can be difficult to achieve. Too many employees working, along with the tools and assets to support the service, and no or low demand leaves resources idle. This is very costly for a company. Too much demand and not enough employees will disappoint customers and result in frustrated customers, complaints, and lost sales.

To measure demand, start by seeking either industry data about peaks and valleys, and source documentation within the company. Next, find methods and attempt to smooth out demand. Schedule appropriately (add extra staff on busy days or seek ways to expand capacity during peak times). For example, airlines price flights occurring in summer or recognized seasonal holidays differently than non peak times, or some companies offer discounts to seniors on Tuesdays. Develop a measurement tool that offers value to the company and does not violate the service delivery model. For example, if the company markets itself as never having to stand in line for a purchase, ensure there is ample staff to manage demand. Measure and monitor.

Sixth, in conjunction with demand management, is the capacity and skills management of the service provider and their employees with their ability to fill the demand. Because services are labor-intensive, intangible, and heterogeneous, an employee working closely with a customer is required to fulfill a level of service and satisfaction for the customer. Therefore, this process includes having the right person or people at the right time to fulfill customer orders, per customer expectations and according to your service delivery model. This requires the right skill or competency.

For some companies, bots (short for "robots," or software applications, programed to execute specific tasks) have replaced customer service representatives which are programed to respond to basic questions from customers (e.g., operating hours at a company). However, when a customer's questions become more complex or specific to their personal needs, the company needs to provide specialized personnel. We have all felt the frustration of an inexperienced salesperson when we have specific needs. In general, service companies begin with less specialized resources and work toward more specialization as the service progresses (or as requested by a customer). For example, junior consultants may review client data and complete an initial analysis before passing it to senior consultants for a review of the work and to provide a deeper analysis.

Lawyers may employ students or newly graduated lawyers to seek out case law. A hospital surgery starts at admittance, and then on to nurses, doctors, anesthetists, and so on.

Skills are one aspect of the people performing the actual service; capacity is another component. A hair stylist can only work with one customer at a time. I am not referring to multitasking. Sure, we can make the company a little more efficient and effective so that a client is getting their hair washed while the hair stylist is cutting another client's hair (less specialized skill to more specialized). However, note that this example demonstrates the hair-cutting experience requires two people—because the capacity of each person is one client at a time. How long it takes each of these people to complete their task(s) is a determinant of productivity. The faster each can complete their tasks (without compromising service delivery), higher productivity is achieved. This will generally relate to profitability and customer satisfaction—so long as an expected level of quality is achieved and maintained. We do not expect the same level of quality from companies such as speedy haircut facilities versus high-end spas or hair salons. Seeking ways to standardize a service and make the service delivery more efficient and effective is an opportunity. This is explored later in this chapter.

The measurement associated with demand management, capacity, and skills management can be highly subjective as it is, in large, based on customer experience. Recall the service supply chain definition introduced earlier; the last sentence included "… have a quality dimension that often is difficult to judge." Two people can engage with the same service delivery person, yet each may have a very different satisfaction level. Typically, only after many encounters can we generalize whether the service delivery person or level received is good or not. Developing an objective means to measure the experience includes suggestions such as repeat clients, referrals, total invoice, and customer service survey results. For the service providers (employees) to perceive they are being treated fairly and equally compared to their peers, there must also be an objective measure to evaluate the level of service provided to customers. When the perceived measurement method is deemed to be reasonably fair, most employees will focus on driving results for their own personal accomplishment and financial or career reward.

Seventh, information flow. Information flow is defined as "the process of linking the participants in the chain through information. It involves collecting and transmitting and processing data to create information to support all the other management processes."[13] This process can provide, for example, valuable information on employee skills (i.e., employee certification or average pay), capacity (i.e., how many customers were served on Friday), customers (i.e., purchasing details and frequency), supplier (i.e., product lists and pricing), and cash flow (i.e., receivables outstanding). Starting with good data is perhaps the most difficult part! Most companies have little reliable data with which to make good value-creating decisions.

Eighth, knowledge management. This includes the creation, storage, and dissemination of company knowledge. In conjunction with information flow, this process examines how much and which information to capture and share within the supply chain. This is a balancing act of cost, time, and value to the company. Good data enable good decisions. However, establishing the ability to capture good data takes time, adds costs to the company, and requires an understanding of privacy acts (and ethics). In the end, most companies use only a fraction of the data they have captured and are still in the learning phase of making good use of the data they do have, which results in expensive data.

Last is risk management. Service supply chains are more complex, non linear, can involve more suppliers and customers, and have long life cycles; all of which can increase the level of risk. Consider a supply chain disruption of a good. If a manufacturing plant has issues, the company has options such as using up stored inventory, outsourcing, or purchasing from a new supplier. However, a supply chain disruption with a service can halt operations. For example, if a lawyer or an accountant becomes sick and is away from the company, depending on the skills and capacity of others, customers may or may not receive service. Note that with these risk examples, other processes such as capacity and demand are also impacted.

Integrating the Service Delivery

While reading through the nine service processes, you may have realized that there is an interdependent relationship between them. How each influences the others and the relationship shared between them is an important factor in the ability for a company to deliver the service as planned. Figure 7.1 lays out the three core units involved in delivering a service: the supplier(s), service provider, and the customer.

The overlapping circles illustrate the direct interaction between the service provider and the customer as the service is provided and consumed simultaneously. It demonstrates the interaction between the supplier and the service provider required in the company's service delivery model. Because primary activities associated with the value chain can occur concurrently in a service, the figure lays out the complexities associated with the timing of when each process is called upon and how each interacts and overlaps with other processes in order to deliver the service. Two of these (service performance management and order process management) have not yet been discussed but will be addressed in the next section.

It can be deduced from the model that delivering a service is not always an easy task. Even more difficult is delivering the service consistently, effectively and efficiently required for value creation. Measuring the value created can be difficult and time and labor-intensive. Measurement can be determined by outputs (e.g., how many oil changes per day) and by outcomes (e.g., average wait times for customers).[15] Outcomes can be measured as hard (e.g., total value of up-selling, such as synthetic oil or oil filters) or soft (e.g., customer service survey results).[15] Because services are generally intangible, it is difficult to measure the effectiveness of the supply chain and where inefficiencies or issues may reside. To minimize these issues, the next section provides the foundation for developing a service strategy.

A Project Approach to Developing a Service Strategy

Because most people stated it can be difficult or very difficult to purchase a service, this section outlines considerations for simplifying

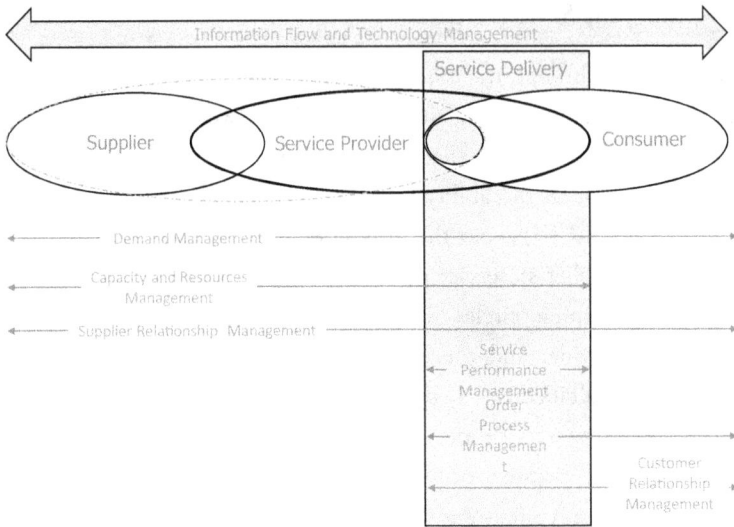

Figure 7.1 Service supply chain

Source: Citation 14—Baltacioglu.

that process. Foundational material from Part 1 of the book is bundled together with research and industry best practices.

Service-based project decisions can include those initiated by a service provider attempting to improve their own service delivery model, or a company may initiate a new service in addition to the products they produce. This section aims to provide the necessary foundation and considerations for making a value-creating project decision. These types of projects are deemed to be projects because the company steps outside of their day-to-day operations.

The goal of the book is to help readers have the necessary background for making value-creating supply chain project decisions. This is described as decisions that expend minimal resources, are made efficiently, and create opportunities or revenue for a company. This is much more difficult to do with a service.

These decisions commence with understanding and applying the material in Part 1 of the book. For example, the vision serves to guide employees and establish expectations as a customer. Further, it provides insight into what the company aims to provide. Referring back to the example of a vision: "To be the premiere shopping destination in the communities we serve" and a mission: "To provide outstanding service, quality products, superior facilities, and exceptional value." How this is accomplished is defined in the service delivery model. For example, outstanding service implies knowledgeable, friendly employees who are available when needed.

Next, define the core service along with how it benefits customers. For example, options for customers having their vehicle oil changed might include a drive-through-while-you-wait oil change; or customers can take their vehicle to the service function of a car dealership and leave it there for the day. With the while-you-wait example, the core service is an oil change based on speed and convenience. With the car dealership example, the core service is a one-stop shop for all vehicle maintenance and mechanical needs, including oil changes.

Next, consider how the company competes in the market: their strategic position. The strategic position for the while-you-wait oil-change type of shops is to be quick, efficient, and reasonably available when needed. These places do not provide a certified mechanic and are not equipped with specialized tools and diagnostic equipment. Their retail sites are located on the corner of a busy street and have only a couple of parking spots (customers do not leave their cars on the property). To compete within this market, the strategic position for one company might be to offer additional products such as synthetic oil, another brand might offer a loyalty program, or another might have longer operating hours.

Any changes to the strategy or strategic position in the market may require changes to the service delivery model, which would initiate a project. Consider who the customer is, what changes are required, how service is presently delivered (service delivery management processes), and how these changes cut across the various functions within the company and suppliers. For example, suppose a while-you-wait oil-change shop implements an online booking option where customers can select from a list of appointment times. This new strategy may require updates to the service delivery model.

Once the core service is clarified along with the strategic position, further flesh out the service delivery components from Figure 7.1.[14] Notice that there are two additional processes which have not yet been addressed: service performance management and order process management. Order process management is the process of mapping how a customer order will be accepted, filled, monitored, and communicated to the customer throughout the service delivery experience. Order process further defines how the company will achieve their strategic position. For example, does the while-you-wait oil-change shop accept orders through an online booking system? Are walk-ins permitted? Phone calls? All of these? Each of these needs to be defined and built into the order process management.

The service performance and order process work in tandem together as follows. Once the order process management is underway, service performance management is initiated.[14] This process focuses on the actual performance of the service—the oil change. Recall performance and consumption occurs simultaneously—the oil change cannot be separated from the service provider and, because a physical good cannot change between buyer and provider, it is impossible to transfer ownership. Once the service performance is complete (the oil change), the order process continues with activities such as payment, a follow-up customer survey, future communication, and CRM. Although the two processes work closely together, it is important to separate them. This is important for measurement and accountability. For example, receiving poor service from a new or disgruntled employee should not represent the customer's entire experience with a company.

Now that the actual service has been defined (the oil change), we can work outward from the actual performance of the service and focus on optimizing the service offering across the service provider and the supply chain. These focus on the marketing and sales processes (value chain primary activity) and the service providers' suppliers and their customers. Each of these is addressed next.

First, demand management. As an example, online oil-change bookings can help secure demand along with the associated number of employees and inventory required for the booked oil changes. Capacity issues can be considered and evaluated. For example, an oil change company with three service bays can allocate two of these for online booking, and the third can be made available for drive-up customers. Incorporate the vision, mission, core service, and the service delivery process to help define and align demand with the resources required for the service.

Second, supplier management. The service delivery model will help define the requirements from suppliers. No supplier can be everything to every company, the focal company must be clear on what their suppliers' needs are to fulfil the service delivery to their customers. Is geographical coverage important? Quality and quality assurance? Lead times and reliability? Reputation and financial stability? Determine the factors that support service delivery and build those into a service-level agreement (SLA). A good SLA starts with the focal company having clear requirements and priorities included in the RFP. This opens the door for qualified suppliers to demonstrate their capability and how they can support service delivery. The SLA should reflect these require-ments and include metrics to measure the service as well as penalties if the SLA is not adhered to. The SLA should also include reporting processes and frequency, dispute resolution process, how service is to be measured. From the suppliers' perspective, services requested outside the SLA should be carefully evaluated—constantly adding additional services (i.e., scope creep) that are not chargeable can become costly for the supplier and may eventually become expected.

Third, customers' perspective. The primary activities in the value chain include marketing and sales. Work closely with the marketing and sales functions to ensure the team understands what is required to successfully deliver the service. This enables the other functions to ensure that the service delivery model is captured in CRM and marketing materials. Adding online booking at the oil-change shop provides an excellent opportunity for reaching the market at large as well as marketing to existing customers. Whatever is committed to the customer in sales and marketing tools first needs to be defined and thought out in the service delivery model and committed to by suppliers.

The steps outlined in this section help create value in a company by making decisions aligned with the company vision, mission, strategic position, goals, and strategy, and building them into processes that support the service delivery. The final section provides recommendations for improving the success of projects pursuing this effort.

Considerations for Service-Based Projects

Now that the differences between goods and services have been discussed, and service processes have been defined including how they integrate with Porter's value chain, this section focuses on consideration of project criteria that are unique to services. What should be obvious at this point is that service delivery, particularly how it is managed and executed, is very different from production of goods.

This section outlines a variety of factors to consider when making service-based value-creating project decisions. It starts with a selection of project management knowledge areas and then moves to additional recommendations for making value-creating decisions that include standardization and continual improvement.

Project Information and Knowledge Areas improving the efficiency and effectiveness

According to the Project Management Institute (PMI), a project can entail a "product, service, or result." Further, the PMI defines a service as "useful *work* performed that does not produce a tangible product or result."[7] A result is defined as "an output from performing project management processes and activities"[7] and includes outcomes and documents. A gap appears to exist in that the PMI literature does not differentiate between managing projects that are product- versus service-based. However, it does recognize the need to adapt projects based on certain criteria. For example, issues such as degree of innovation, requirements certainty (when the project requirements are well known and easy to define), scope stability, and ease of change when the nature of the deliverable makes it difficult to manage—all require adaptations as to how the project is managed.[16] Finally, the

PMI acknowledges certain organizational factors such as culture and organizational capability that again require changes to how the project is managed.

Because service-based projects are unique, processes must be adapted to each project. Recall earlier in this chapter, a landscaping project was discussed which noted the flow between project, suppliers, and customers and the potential for scope changes. Issues like this are not unique in a service-based project. Therefore, when a company develops (or alters) their service delivery model, they must consider the various impacts of how the service is executed as laid out in the service supply chain model. Seven knowledge areas are addressed here along with other key project considerations. Your project might require some or all of these knowledge areas. This reflects the uniqueness and complexity involved with managing a service-based project.

First, integration management. This is a critical component supporting the ability of a service-based company to deliver their service. Integration activities begin by focusing on how the company will bring together the various service processes as laid out in the service supply chain model. It should start with a review of service performance management and order process management, required for service delivery. The necessary steps, timing, and resource requirements need to be clearly described, as well as how and when these intersect and integrate with suppliers and customers. They help define the requirements and expectations for both supplier and customer contracts.

A simple example of integration: if Amazon states they provide 24-hour, guaranteed service delivery with goods purchased online, then Amazon must work with their suppliers to integrate processes and information flow to push the order to suppliers within a certain time frame—as agreed upon by the supplier and Amazon. Without the necessary infrastructure and integration, the supplier is unable to support Amazon's service delivery model. This requirement should be included in the RFP and validated during the due diligence process. Next, this becomes the measurement upon which the service level agreement is based.

It is easy to see why integration activities should encompass stakeholders with both primary and support activities, including intracompany and external (i.e., customers and suppliers). Early and ongoing engagement must be done with the project sponsor and the primary stakeholders as they will be impacted by the service supply chain project. They may have changes to their jobs, the technology they use, and the processes they use to complete their work. In order to be ready to accept the change associated with the project, an integration plan needs to be developed.

The second knowledge area is project scope management: identifying the work required to complete the project and achieve the goals (purpose) of the project. The work breakdown structure (WBS) represents the work required to complete in order to enable the service delivery model. For example, a project aimed at increasing the capacity of the service provider's facility will be reflected in the WBS. Identifying and working closely with stakeholders through the design (and execution) phase is critical to ensuring that once the project is complete, the service delivery is enabled according to plan. Creating a WBS may require an agile approach to service-based projects (not covered in this book).

Third, the WBS is foundational for producing a schedule. Given the intangible nature of a service, the WBS will be a critical tool to support building the schedule and serve as a useful tool to manage communication with stakeholders, including suppliers.

The work packages from the WBS will be used to support the fourth knowledge area: procurement. Contracting a service requires special attention. This includes sourcing suppliers that support the project goals and can demonstrate how they will support the delivery of the service. Recall in the value chain model that procurement is a critical support activity which can support the achievement of value-creating project decisions.

Fifth, quality. With both quality and services being such abstract concepts, each must be made "tangible." The service provider must define what quality means to the company—it is their strategic position. For instance, in the previous example of Amazon, delivering within

24 hours is a quality statement. How the quality statement will be achieved will be mapped out within the order and service processes. The "while-you-wait" oil-change example might define quality as the ability to meet all online appointments or have a specified customer wait time. Value-creating decisions ensure that the quality specified is aligned with company policies, such as regulatory and safety, in order to protect people and the community and maintain the company's reputation.

Sixth, effective project communication is perhaps even more important with a service versus a product project. The WBS serves as an important communication tool which helps project team members communicate scope, schedule, and cost. Ensure a needs assessment has been completed early in the project to identify stakeholder and, especially, customer requirements. A business readiness plan linking the project to the service delivery model should be reviewed by the service provider and signed off. Ongoing communication should focus on the project progression and include how stakeholder needs are being achieved.

Risk is the final knowledge area to consider. Ensure the risk management processes recommended earlier in the book are followed. In addition to this, perhaps the biggest risk is giving a service "tangibility" so that project members understand all of the deliverables and their importance to project success. Again, clearly articulating the service delivery model and how each of the other services' processes are to be accomplished should be reflected in the project deliverables.

Standardization and Continuous Improvement

Value-creating decisions find ways of increasing productivity (and ultimately profitability) without compromising the quality and reputation of the company or impacting sales. Therefore, service-based projects can be based upon improving the efficiency and effectiveness of the service. Projects should also include examining methods to standardize the service delivery.

A "standard" can be defined as a "norm" your company must meet each time. Standardization refers to the steps that make the service delivery consistent and repeatable for customers. It focuses on replicating a process each time. For example, following opening and closing procedures consistently at a business. Earlier in the chapter, a hospital surgery example was cited where the patient begins the process in admittance where personal information and other information such as medical insurance is validated. The expectation is every employee follows the same process each time service is delivered.

One of the benefits of standardization is a decrease in labor effort and customer interaction.[17] It can be a method for decreasing cost while improving productivity. For example, a law office would have a standard contract for a will that could be applied to all their clients. However, the lawyer will seek individual information from each client to populate the contract (e.g., children, assets, pension, and so on). With this example, the law firm can increase capacity and accept more clients while still offering value to them. In fact, most clients would appreciate a law firm approaching this process in an efficient and effective manner (lower cost, faster) while still individualizing the will reflecting personal client information. Any process which increases productivity is a value-creating decision because it can increase profitability, but never at the risk of impacting quality and company reputation.

With our wills and estate example, it is inefficient and unnecessary to draft a contract from scratch for each client. There are situations when a standard contact would be applicable. However, in situations where a client requires a lawyer for a unique, one-time criminal or corporate issue, the process is unique and is not repeatable. Some qualifiers make this possible and help determine the level of standardization a company pursues, that is, the amount of labor required, and the degree of customer interaction and customization.[17]

First, the amount of labor required to produce the service will vary depending on the service and the service delivery model. For example, as a passenger on an airplane, I require very little labor from the stewards. Conversely, a haircut cannot be performed without the hair stylist. Automation is having a big impact on labor. For example, robots can now cook a burger at a fast-food restaurant. Think of the advantage— the robot can be programed to flip burgers at a specific time interval, ensuring no under- or overcooked product. A robot does not call in sick and always feels like working. In this example, the service can be standardized, for a cost. And while there are other issues that can occur (e.g., the machine breaks down), it resolves, or minimizes, the need for labor. Technology and automation are changing how we think about the amount of labor required in ways we could have never imagined. Autonomous vehicles are another example—while today this is not fully possible, or safe, at some point this scenario will probably be a reality. Other services might always require a high degree of labor—only a tailor can alter and fit a suit to the customer perfectly, or a criminal lawyer mount a defense in the courtroom.

The second criterion: the degree of customer interaction and customization. The introduction of self-checkout at retail stores has demonstrated that, in certain situations, some customers prefer less interaction in exchange for efficiency and effectiveness. Other services require a higher level of interaction—the tailor must meet with the client to take measurements and discuss alterations requested by the customer (customization) before performing the service work (amount of labor).

Standardization can occur when it is possible to decrease the amount of labor required for the service along with the amount of customer interaction. Let's assume that a robot will cook and flip burgers at a fast-food restaurant. This process can minimize the labor required and all but eliminate any customization. Standardizing this is a value-creating decision because the quality will be consistent and minimize safety concerns. Labor is still required for assembling the burger and for any customization requested by the customer (assuming this is possible in the service delivery model).

The final consideration for a service strategy is to incorporate a continual improvement mindset in the corporate culture. A continual improvement approach aims to seek opportunities to streamline and improve how the product or service is being manufactured or provided to customers, along with the associated processes. All companies should encourage employees to seek projects which support more efficient ways to "do more with less" as it relates to the service delivery. Front line employees are in an ideal position to receive feedback from customers and discuss with leaders. Often these same front line employees know the frustration of a bottleneck and are more than willing to provide suggestions on how their job could be streamlined. Small tweaks can result in significant savings and improved service for customers, without compromising quality or safety.

Summary

Services constitute the majority of everything a developed country produces. The process of managing a service is typically very different than managing the manufacturing of a product. Most people in management state that it is difficult or very difficult to manage a service. Given this, we would assume that best practices exist on how to effectively manage services. While some excellent research exists, along with some best-practices information we've explored, in general, opportunities remain to better understand and manage services.

For now, to effectively manage a service, research and recommendations include the following. First, understand the key differences between providing a service and a product. Six criteria were discussed to showcase these differences and how they make it more difficult to effectively deliver a service to customers.

Second, Porter's value chain provides a visual of where and how the value is created in a company, including the primary activities that generally occur in a linear process. Conversely, because a service is both created for the customer and consumed at the same time, the value chain activities occur concurrently. Therefore, unique processes have been developed to help articulate how the service can be best delivered. The service supply chain provides a visual of service delivery, including the processes required to deliver value.

Finally, to manage a service-based project, start with the company's vision, mission, strategy, and strategic position in the market. This will be a guide to how to think about the service delivery model, including ways to improve the efficiency and effectiveness of service delivery. Improving how services are delivered includes standardization and continual improvement—both helping to improve productivity and, ultimately, profitability by seeking efficiencies and improving the effectiveness of the service.

Application Questions

1. Given the prevalence of services in western countries, explain why they are still so difficult to manage.
2. Explain the importance of the primary activity of sales and marketing to a service.
3. Define how service processes are aligned with Porter's value chain.
4. Explain how a company's strategic position relates to their service delivery.
5. Explain how service projects can be effectively managed.
6. Explain the importance of a standard and how a standard can be used to create efficiencies with a service-based company.
7. Discuss how a standard and quality are similar. Discuss how they differ.

CHAPTER 8

Conclusion of Value-Creating Project Supply Chain Decisions

Most people spend more time and energy going around problems than in trying to solve them.

—Henry Ford

The intent of this book is to guide readers toward making decisions. The goal is to provide a foundation for what goes into making a good supply chain project decision. It is not meant to be a comprehensive source of information for educating readers about everything associated with the discipline of supply chain. There are many great books on the topic.

The information presented in this book can be applied to almost any supply chain topic, such as sourcing raw materials, logistics, distribution, and warehousing. For example, a project decision focusing on warehousing is a service decision. Services are discussed in Chapter 7. For another example, a project centered on building a new distribution center or leasing space from a supplier is covered in Chapter 6—make or buy. In essence, most supply chain decisions can be linked back to the foundational topics discussed within this book. Part 1 of the book provides the necessary framework, information, and guidance to make a good decision. Part 2 focuses on two of the most difficult types of supply chain decisions to be made: services and make or buy decisions. The material within is intended to guide all facets of supply chain project decisions.

Learning how to make a good decision is not typically a skill taught in post secondary school or in the workplace. Good decision making is a skill learned over time. It is a key skill companies recruit for.

Companies look for a candidate's ability to identify problems within the supply chain, to develop solutions, to have a method for organizing the solution, and to communicate this to stakeholders. Further, companies want employees to have the capability of sourcing data, identifying trends, and seeking opportunities to create efficiencies, cost savings, or increased quality; in essence, seeking out value-creating opportunities. This is the focus of the book.

In Chapter 2, the five phases of a project are laid out. Once the project has been operationalized, the project will be officially closed. Reflecting on the project's success and generating a list of lessons learned is an important endeavor for this phase. This final chapter provides lessons learned and recommendations for further development of decision making skills.

Conclusions and Lessons Learned

The following list summarizes the key points of the book and explains the relevance of the material. Included is a perspective on how the material may be applied in a company in any industry.

Supply Chain Project Decisions

Decision making can be difficult and complex. I have seen many leaders who refuse to make them. Think about this: if you never make a decision, you cannot be held accountable for it. How is this done? Some leaders will stall and stall. They might send your project proposal back because it has a few errors—and then stall again when you resubmit it. Or they might say they are waiting for more information or that it is on someone else's desk to review. Sadly, failing to make a decision is not a rare occurrence in business.

Why might leaders do this? For a variety of reasons, many of which will have nothing to do with you or your proposal. For example, your priorities may not align with your leaders' priorities. Or they might not see the value of your project (hint: ensure you position your project as "what's in it for them and for the company"—not for you or how it makes your work easier). There could be similar or competing projects circulating at a more senior level that you are not privy to. Also, some projects can be very political. Perhaps, the company strategy might be changing. Or there might be issues occurring which cannot be disclosed to all employees until a later date (e.g., leaders working through an acquisition or layoffs impending). The culture of the company might not be conducive to decision making (e.g., people are chastised for their decisions). At times, decision making takes courage.

For the decisions you will be responsible for in your job, you will never have all the data required to make a "perfect" decision. Hence, there is no such thing as a perfect decision. The decision needs to be made with the best possible information, with limited resources, and tight time constraints.

The opportunity for you is to gather as much relevant data as you can and follow the recommendations within this book on how to make a decision. Seek input from the sponsor and key stakeholders. Ensure you understand what is important to the company, such as strategy and risk tolerance. Then make the best possible decision you can.

As a project progresses, if you realize that the project idea might not be feasible, admit defeat and pull the plug (stop the project). Do not continue to defend the indefensible. Doing so prolongs the inevitable and may impact your reputation in the company. People will respect you for recognizing the need to stop the project rather than continuing to maintain that the project will benefit the company. This is, of course, assuming your original project decision was based on the best possible information at the time. But things happen; the competitive landscape changes, budgets and priorities change. Move on when necessary. However, if your project progresses according to the project plan and proves successful, take the win and enjoy the achievement!

Value-Creating Project Decisions

Value-creating decisions are the "next level" of good decision making. Recall the maturity model introduced in Chapter 4. It was noted that most companies operate at a maturity level of 1 or 2. Initially, so too will most of your decisions. Good decision making takes time, experience, a good understanding of how things get done in your company, and having a keen eye for an opportunity. As the saying goes: You must crawl before you can walk. Actions you can take to get better at identifying opportunities are provided in this section.

Be great at knowing everything you can about your current position. Understand why the company does what it does and how it creates value. If you have responsibility for a budget and profit and loss (P&L) statements—sit with your accounting partner and know what makes up every single line item on the reports. For example, my P&L statements always had a line item called "banking fees." This line included monthly charges from the bank, credit card fees paid to the major credit card companies, and a cents per transaction for each debit card use. Breaking this down at one company, I saw we were paying the bank 12 cents per customer transaction; I knew this could easily be negotiated to 9 cents. Think of the savings! Multiply 3 cents by the transactions per day, times how many retail sites across a network, times 365 days per year. This was an opportunity to create value. Even if this cannot be renegotiated, having this information allows a business to look at other options such as providing a discount for customers using cash. Or the fee could be passed on to customers. The more you know and compare your company information to industry standards, the more you will see where opportunities reside.

Read your company reports and budgets. There should be lots of information available for publicly traded and nonprofit companies or if you work for the local, provincial (state), or federal level of government. Use these reports to identify and understand why the leaders have taken the direction they have (i.e., goals, projects, priorities, and so on). Be familiar with the culture of your company and the risk tolerance level. Projects that are too risky for your company will probably not be considered.

Be great at what you are doing no matter what the role is. I hear students who take a co-op position or are in their first job, and they say, "It's just a ..." (fill in the blank—the company or the role is not prestigious enough, or it does not have a great title). It is never "just a"; it is an honest day of work for an honest day of pay. Be proud. Learn and ask questions. I guarantee that whatever you do, the role will contribute to your foundation of information on which to base great decisions as your career progresses.

Value Chain Optimization

Companies where employees seek the contribution of other functions often operate more efficiently and effectively. Forge cross-boundary relationships with colleagues and try to understand the contribution and goals of each function. Seek to comprehend how each creates value, including the methods and processes they use to do it. Follow the business processes across primary and support functions; where and how does each add value? Because the primary value chain members are the functions that drive revenue in a company, they will naturally be the primary project instigators and usually first to receive project approval. The more you understand about your company, the easier it will be to make supply chain project decisions that benefit the company, not just your work unit.

Sometimes the most valuable people in a company are those who have been there for decades. They know where every form can be found and how to fill it in. They know all the employees in a company and are excellent at managing the politics. They can provide lots of useful information on how to get things approved in a company and why the company does things in a particular way. Conversely, other valuable people are employees who are new to a company. They can quickly see where opportunity resides based on their previous, extensive experience. But for these new employees to be successful in the company, they first need to understand how the company creates value. Understanding the culture will provide insight into how to successfully manage stakeholders. Recently, I was at a data management conference. One of the speakers stated that "until you connect the dots and understand each function's business challenges, you cannot solve the problem." Companies operate as a system; understanding how it produces goods and services will open the door to value-creating decisions.

Project Management

Projects differ from the day-to-day operations. They can change the face of a company and alter how the company creates value. Furthermore, a project can impact people, their livelihood, their families along with the community a company operates within. Recall the definition of "decision": "irrevocable allocation of resources."[1] Once initiated, a project requires resources of time, people, money, and assets, all of which cannot be replaced.

Smaller projects are defined as those that impact a single function and do not radically alter how theCompanies where employees seek the co business creates their goods and services. These are great learning opportunities for new employees, individual contributors, or junior managers. Major, company-changing projects, such as an acquisition or a new Enterprise Resource Planning (ERP) software, are often politically charged. Academic research suggests that these must be initiated by senior leaders in a company.[2] This is because for a major project to get traction within a company, it requires the ability to influence key stakeholders across the company. It requires buy-in and commitment from leaders who will most likely have competing projects.

I offer some recommendations on how to improve project success—outside of the project itself. First, ask your leader to recommend your name for company wide projects. Conversely, if your leader asks you to reside on a company wide project, it is a good sign they see value in your people skills, given their request to represent your function.

Second, to initiate a project, be clear on how your project concept will help the company achieve its strategy (I did not ask how will it help you or your function). Seek to understand why the project concept had not been initiated before. Have clear project goals that your leader supports and will endorse. Clearly outline how the project will create value in the company.

Third, complete a stakeholder impact assessment early in the process. Knowing how the project will alter the work of other employees and stakeholders will provide additional insight and guidance.

Last, if your leader takes credit for the project, so be it. Let it go. If you want the project badly enough to make your work life easier, then let the leader take the credit. Of course, I hope they do not, but it is a distinct possibility they will.

Measurement

Measurement is important to demonstrate we have accomplished what we intended. In life, we measure many things—our weight, the speed we are driving, our age, the grade on an exam. In business, we measure profit margin, market share, and an increase or decrease in sales.

With a project, the goals may be stated, but often the plan lacks a method to measure goal achievement. Rarely, will companies measure project (and operational) results against the goals. Or they may initially but fail to track over time. Measurement is important to solidify whether the goal was achieved. What if we failed to measure important stuff in our life? For example, what if our goal is to bake a beautiful birthday cake, but we choose not to measure the ingredients and instead just put them all in at once—how well would the cake turn out? It would not. Or, if a doctor writes a prescription but fails to provide the measurement for the specific patient? There needs to be a valid and reliable method of measurement, then, at some point (or at multiple points), measuring to determine if the goal was achieved. Measurement helps the project instigator determine if the project was a good decision.

Measurement is an important component in the learning process. Recall in Chapter 3 and in Chapter 5 that receiving feedback on our decisions is necessary to becoming good decision makers. Chapter 5 also addresses how risk relates to learning. It can be risky to our learning process to not receive feedback. Without it, we may be misguided as to the effectiveness of our decisions. We will have "bad data" for future similar decisions. Therefore, measuring is vital to our learning and professional development. In business, all employees should meet with their leader to receive a review of their work over a specified time (6–12 months) (note, however, even more important is receiving ongoing feedback!). This is the performance management process. Unfortunately, some companies have a flawed process of what and how they measure employee performance. Further, the capability of some leaders to conduct a valid, reliable review of each employee has its share of issues.

Good data are foundational to good decision making. Bad data can lead to poor decisions. Good projects and project goals are founded on good data. Seek a simple, relevant, and accurate method to measure supply chain projects.

Business Processes

When we first start in a job, business processes help us understand how to get work done. For example, processes guide us in completing our monthly expenses. They help us order supplies. They help us book our holidays and document a sick day. They guide customers in how to purchase a product from our company. Some business processes are documented, others are undocumented, and they reflect a workaround of how to get work done. Each of these provides a level of standardization ensuring everyone completes the same repetitive task in a similar manner. Companies have hundreds of processes. These move across functions and can extend into the supply chain with customers and suppliers.

Initially, you will find processes provide a roadmap to help you get your work done efficiently. Culture can dictate how work gets done in a company. Culture can impact safety or have other unintended consequences (e.g., "no one wears safety equipment around here"). You may also find that some of the processes might lose value for the company because they are inefficient. For example, the credit application process might be very cumbersome or take too long to receive approval. Recognizing inefficiencies in a business process and initiating an action to rework a process may indicate you are applying the lessons in this book and working to create value for your company and customers. Recall the Dreyfus and Dreyfus model from Chapter 3—your project indicates you are moving from a novice (stage 1) and advanced beginner (stage 2) into competence (stage 3) or proficiency with your work (stage 4) and that you understand the definition of value-creating decisions.

Consider the maturity model—this may indicate your ability to create value across primary activities. This is where the supply chain project opportunity begins!

In addition to rethinking the processes across the value chain, there are other helpful tools, processes, and models which challenge us to think differently about our work or which stimulate innovation. Models such as a SWOT (strengths, weaknesses, opportunities, and threats) or a Pareto chart help us to recognize opportunities in our company.

Risk and Opportunity

For the last couple of decades, most companies directed their supply chain management efforts on cost-cutting efforts and being "lean." For example, in one large company I worked in, each sub function contracted with a local travel agency to make travel arrangements. The number of agencies was over 50. Consider the cost savings in reducing this to just one agency! The ability to negotiate one contract and make one payment to one supplier. This was only one supplier of hundreds across the company. The opportunity to provide value was immense.

Initiatives such as this along with others, such as offshore manufacturing or global sourcing of parts, lead to having a centralized procurement function and an increased role for supply chain management in many companies. Outsourcing both primary and support activities with the goal of cutting costs has become easier and more common. Globalization and technology enable even small companies to participate in cost-cutting initiatives.

Initiatives also include companies seeking to collect good data used in making effective decisions. While technology has progressed significantly in the last few years, issues exist with obtaining good data. Further, endeavors to link supply chain partners together with technology and data sharing are proving difficult and have introduced new risks.

A recent increase in supply chain upsets (e.g., Covid-19) has resulted in companies not delivering products and services to their customers. Efforts to make supply chains more effective and efficient are proving challenging to execute smoothly and with low risk.

The current shift is to rethink the supply chain strategy. After all—if you do not have it, you cannot sell it. Shifting from a supply chain strategy focused mainly on efficiency and cost-cutting, the direction for many companies is now focused on "supply chain resilience." Resilience is defined as "a systems ability to absorb change."[3] In other words, supply chain upsets are inevitable; building capacity to prevent or support operational upsets is now the goal for many companies. This requires that a company have a means for ensuring incidents, or change, have a minimal impact on operations, the value chain, and the value chain system. Therefore, the opportunity for supply chain employees is to initiate projects that ensure resilience to protect or create value and reduce risk.

Finally, recall that risk has its root in perception. Our perceptions can introduce bias. This may cause us to make decisions that are not based on facts. As a result, our decisions may not be sound. Our perceptions and proposed decisions should be checked against facts, along with seeking opinions and input from other data sources.

Other Material Not in the Book—And Why

This section presents a brief overview of other important topics not covered in this book, yet which are relevant to good supply chain decision making. First, ethics. Having an ethical model that guides our ability to make good decisions is obviously very important. However, writing on the topic of ethics is not in my wheelhouse. So I provide some guidance below on how to tackle this subject along with reading material from an author who covers this topic much more effectively than I can. The other three topics addressed in this section (sustainability, technology, and data management) are all relevant to making a good decision, but I consider to be secondary to having a foundation in good decision making. I offer my thoughts and some suggested readings below. And I encourage you to continue to build your foundation in value-creating supply chain decision making through courses and published reading material from research and industry associations.

Ethics

Value-creating decisions that expend a minimal number of resources are done in an efficient manner, and they create opportunities or revenue for a company. In Chapter 1, I noted value-creating decisions must be done safely, must follow all laws, and must be done ethically. But what exactly is a "good" ethical decision? Many business schools teach students to approach the topic as a rational decision where the facts are weighed, and the best solution is actioned. Unfortunately, this does little to prepare students for what is the "best" solution, especially because the options might conflict with each other, or experience, or bias, and so on, may make it not obvious which of the options is a good or ethical decision.

I highly recommend a succinct, informative, easy-to-read, and compelling book, *How to Be Profitable and Moral*, by Jaana Woiceshyn. Dr. Woiceshyn provides a practical approach to making ethical decisions. In addition, the book provides a variation on what it means to make a supply chain decision that is both profitable (value-creating) and ethical.

Woiceshyn, J. 2011. *How to Be Profitable and Moral: A Rational Egoist Approach to Business*. Landham, MD: Hamilton Books.

Sustainability

Another important supply chain management topic receiving a lot of attention from both academics and within the workplace is sustainability. Sustainability has been defined by the United Nations (UN) as "meeting the needs of the present without compromising the ability of future generations to meet their own needs."[4] Further, the UN defines sustainable development as an integrated approach that takes into consideration environmental concerns and economic development. This suggests that sustainable decisions can also be value-creating supply chain project decisions. Where and how a company sources inputs, how these are transformed, and the relationships they have with their suppliers and customers are all important factors in supply chain sustainability.

Sustainability can be a highly complex issue, especially for supply chain decision making. Here's an example: one of the assignments I give to my students is to research a supply chain sustainability topic. Students research and write a report that includes the current supply chain practice, the policy or laws (either local or global) governing the practice, a discussion of any existing or proposed technology that is either positively impacting or could impact the supply chain sustainability issue, and finally, based on their research, provide a recommendation. Every year, I am amazed by the topics the students study and their analysis. Some topics prove to be very positive—such as the recent global direction away from bunker fuel used in cargo ships (although it will have an economic impact on fuel pricing).

However, most of their projects outline the difficulty associated with sustainability and supply chain decision making. For example, one group of students studied coffee cups used at coffee shops. Their research found that 500,000 trees are cut down each year in Canada to produce the disposable cups. A cup is used, on average, for 14 minutes before being disposed of. At present, they are lined with a paraffin wax, which is a by-product of petroleum, to keep the hot liquid from soaking through the cup. The wax prevents the cup from being biodegradable. On average, each cup is used for 14 minutes. An alternative is for customers to supply their own reusable cup (some shops provide a slight discount for this). The students' research found that a customer must present the same reusable cup every day for 3 years to "break-even" with the resources and energy required to produce that cup. The technology under development is the application of a sugary wax, which would make the cup fully recyclable. However, at present, this product melts when the cup contains a hot liquid, thereby making the cup unusable for hot liquids.

This simple example demonstrates the complexity associated with sustainability and supply chain decisions. What is the answer to a sustainability problem such as this? Here are some suggestions. First, a continuing focus on technology. Second, a balanced policy between economic and environmental concerns leading to both efficiencies and sustainability goals. Third, using Woiceshyn's book as a helpful roadmap for making ethical decisions (see the Ethics section).

Finally, for readers to round out their education and understanding of sustainability, there is an abundance of reading material available. Read and learn, but also ensure that you understand the complexity of the issue, such as demonstrated in the simple example of disposable coffee cups. And look for material that provides an economic and sustainable solution and does not just offer scare tactics. Further, many of the solutions just shift the existing problem to a new one and "green wash" it to make us believe the change is for the better, such as using our own coffee cups.

Technology

A few comments about technology. First, in general, technology is very expensive. Second, it can take months or years to make a good technology decision for a business. Third, once a decision is made, generally it will take years to implement (which suggests the technology will probably already be outdated). My experience with a handful of ERP software decisions is that from decision to implementation takes between 4 and 8 years.

Last, technology is not, and was never meant to be, the answer to a business problem. The purpose of a digital transformation is to support the achievement of a strategy. I continue to see leaders who spend time with technology vendors who show them shiny toys (technology) and all the "magical" things that technology can do for them. Leaders become totally enamored with the technology and imagine how it would help them. They are sold and sign up for the new technology (refer to the data section for the impact of this approach).

Selecting new technology has little to do with the actual technology; the process must start with strategy (Chapter 4). What is the company trying to accomplish? Only with this goal and direction (strategy) can a company eventually determine which technology will help support the endeavor. Without this approach, the shiny new toy will be nothing more than an expensive new toy. Start with strategy.

One avenue where technology can help is with end-to-end visibility into the supply chain network. Technology can speed up this process and provide a value chain (and value system) comprehensive view of how all the parts link together. Chapter 1 noted business is moving faster and faster every year with no expectation of the pace slowing down. This is in addition to an increasing number of supply chain disruptions. Technology can provide quick, real-time access into the value chain and value system. Again, this initiative must adhere to goals and strategy; the technology only serves to enable this.

Data

Data and artificial intelligence are often lumped together with technology, but should not be. These are two separate functions which may share a symbiotic relationship. Data can have nothing to do with technology. Every business has a lot of data which does not require technology to manage or share it. A simple example: a server at a restaurant might know the same couple (and their preferences) who have frequented the restaurant every Monday night for a year (this is data). Or an accounting firm knows that one of their largest clients always disputes the invoice and takes months to pay. Both are examples of data that do not require technology to know. Data can be an asset to the company. Data can have bias. Data can be stored and mined to be used for decision making. Do not mix up data with technology.

One more note on technology as it relates to data. At present, many companies are moving very fast with technology and are not considering the data associated with the technology. Generally, we have a lack of understanding and respect for the data component. We just expect our data function colleagues to easily source and provide "perfect" data associated with dozens (if not hundreds) of technology platforms. Good data management starts with a data strategy—which, again, must be aligned with company strategy.

Also, ask what data are collected and why—how will it help support achievement of the strategy? Many companies will state much of their data have low to no validity or reliability. Compounding this, many companies are in a rush to collect large amounts of data, yet most companies use less than 10 percent of their data. Data storage can be expensive. This is a good place to mention that data storage (and technology) is trending as an environmental issue as it requires large amounts of energy. Therefore, readers wanting to take a sustainable approach to business should consider the impact of data and technology on their supply chain project decisions.

To do more reading on data and its importance, I recommend the following books:

Aiken, P. and T. Harbour. 2017. *Data Strategy and the Enterprise Data Executive: Ensuring That Business and IT Are in Synch in the Post–Big Data Era*. Technics Publications.

Laney, D.B. 2017. *Infonomics: How to Monetize, Manage, and Measure Information as an Asset for Competitive Advantage*. Routledge.

Summary—What Does It All Mean?

First, have a definite, clear practical ideal; a goal, an objective. Second, have the necessary means to achieve your ends; wisdom, money, materials, and methods. Third, adjust all your means to that end.

—Aristotle

The major reason for setting a goal is for what it makes of you to accomplish it. What it makes of you will always be the far greater value than what you get.

—Jim Rohn

Reading through the list of conclusions and lessons learned in this book should demonstrate a common theme—all the lessons share a symbiotic relationship. What does this mean? It means that you cannot be successful with just one of these—you need them all to build a foundation which is required to make good, value-creating supply chain project decisions. Complex, multi functional problems require a multi dimensional approach. This is only one approach. Big data analytics is another example. Going forward, I suggest we need to rethink about how we tackle these complex problems and projects. For example, more multi disciplinary research by academics and efforts to "de-silo" a company for industry leaders.

Finally, my hope is there have been a few good morsels within the pages of this book that have helped you, the reader, to think about your work and decisions a little differently. Reach out across the boundaries and get to know what others are doing in your company and community. May all your decisions in life and work be value-creating decisions! I leave you with one last quote:

Every new beginning comes from some other beginning's end.

—Seneca

References

Chapter 1

1. Brewer, P.C. and T.W. Speh. 2000. "Using the Balance Scorecard to Measure Supply Chain Performance." *Journal of Business Logistics* 21, no. 1, pp. 75–93.
2. Mentzer, J.T., W. DeWitt, J.S. Keebler, S. Min, N.W. Nix, C.D. Smith, and Z.G. Zacharaia. 2001. "Defining Supply Chain Management." *Journal of Business Logistics* 22, no. 2, pp. 1–26. Page 18.
3. Baltacioglu, T., E. Ada, M. Kaplan, O. Yurt and Y.C. Kaplan. 2007. "A New Framework for Service Supply Chains." *Service Industries Journal* 27, no. 2, pp. 105–124.
4. Bickel, J.E. and R.B. Bratvold, 2008. "From Uncertainty Quantification to Decision Making in the Oil and Gas Industry." *Energy Exploration & Exploitation* 26, no. 5, pp. 311–325.

Chapter 2

1. Porter, M.E. 1985. In *The Competitive Advantage: Creating and Sustaining Superior Performance*. Free Press.
2. Barney, J. and W. Hesterly. 2012. In *Strategic Management and Competitive Advantage,* 305. 4th ed. Pearson.
3. Baltacioglu, T., E. Ada, M. Kaplan, O. Yurt, and Y.C. Kaplan. 2007. "A New Framework for Service Supply Chains." *Service Industries Journal* 27, no. 2, pp. 105–124.
4. Coyle, J.J., E.J. Bardi, and C.J. Langley. 2003. The Management of Business Logistics. 7th ed. Mason.
5. PMI. 2004. In *A Guide to the Project Management Body of Knowledge*, 5–8. 3rd ed. PMI Press.
6. PMI. 2023. In *Process Groups: A Practice Guide*. Independent Publisher Group.
7. PMI. 2004. In *A Guide to the Project Management Body of Knowledge*, 157. 3rd ed. PMI Press.

8. PMI. 2004. In *A Guide to the Project Management Body of Knowledge*, 371. 3rd ed. PMI Press.

9. PMI. 2023. In *Process Groups: A Practice Guide,* 340. Independent Publisher Group.

10. PMI. 2004. In *A Guide to the Project Management Body of Knowledge*, 237, 3rd ed. PMI Press.

11. PMI. 2004. In *A Guide to the Project Management Body of Knowledge*, 368. 3rd ed. PMI Press.

Chapter 3

1. Deming, D.J. 2021. "The Growing Importance of Decision-Making on the Job." National Bureau of Economic Research Working Paper Series, Working Paper No. 28733, 55.

2. Certo, T.S., B.L. Connelly, and L. Tihanyi. 2008. "Managers and Their Not-So Rational Decisions." *Business Horizons* 51, no. 2, pp. 113–119.

3. Deming, D.J. 2021. "The Growing Importance of Decision Making on the Job." National Bureau of Economic Research Working Paper Series, Working paper No. 28733, 55, p. 7.

4. Elliott, J.C. and T.J. Elliott. 2005. In *Decision DNA: Discovering Reality Based Decision Making*, 44. Infinity Publishing.

5. Bickel, J.E. and R.B. Bratvold. 2008. "From Uncertainty Quantification to Decision Making in the Oil and Gas Industry." *Energy Exploration & Exploitation* 26, no. 5, pp. 311–325.

6. Hodgkinson, G.P., J. Langan-Fox, and E. Sadler-Smith. 2008. "Intuition: A Fundamental Bridging Construct in the Behavioural Sciences." *British Journal of Psychology* 99, no. 1, pp. 1–27.

7. Dreyfus, H.L. and S.E. Dreyfus. 2005. "Expertise in Real World Contexts." *Organization Studies* 26, no. 5, pp. 779–792.

8. Epstein, D. 2019. In *Range: Why Generalists Triumph in a Specialized World*, 339. NY, New York: Riverhead Books.

9. Chenger, D. and J. Woiceshyn. 2021. "Executives' Decision Processes at the Front End of Major Projects: The Role of Context and Experience in Value Creation." *Project Management Journal* 52, no 2, pp. 176–191.

Chapter 4

1. Bickel, J.E. and R.B. Bratvold. 2008. "From Uncertainty Quantification to Decision Making in the Oil and Gas Industry." *Energy Exploration & Exploitation* 26, no. 5, pp. 311–325.
2. Crossan, M.M.,M.J. Rouse, J.P. Killing, and J.N. Fry. 2002. In *Strategic Analysis and Action.* Toronto: Prentice Hall.
3. Neely, A., M. Gregory, and K. Platts. 1995. "Performance Measurement System Design." *International Journal of Operations & Production Management* 15, no. 4, p. 80.
4. Mentzer, J.T., W. DeWitt, J.S. Keebler, S. Min, N.W. Nix, C.D. Smith, and Z.G. Zacharia. 2001. "Defining Supply Chain Management." *Journal of Business Logistics* 22, no. 2, p. 18. pp. 1–26.
5. Kaplan, R.S. and D.P. Norton. 1996. "Using the Balanced Scorecard as a Strategic Management System." *Harvard Business Review* 74, no. 1, pp. 75–85.
6. Estampe, D., S. Lamouri, J. L. Paris, and S. Brahim-Djelloul. 2013. "A Framework for Analysing Supply Chain Performance Evaluation Models." *International Journal of Production Economics* 142, no. 2, pp. 247–258.
7. Chia, A., M. Goh, and H. Sin-Hoon. 2009. "Performance Measurement in Supply Chain Entities: Balanced Scorecard Perspective." *Benchmarking* 16, no. 5, pp. 605–620.
8. Maestrini, V., D. Luzzini, P. Maccarone, and F. Caniato. 2017. "Supply Chain Performance Measurement Systems: A Systematic Review and Research Agenda." *International Journal of Production Economics* 183, no. Part A, pp. 299–315.
9. Elliott, J.C. and T.J. Elliott 2005. In *Decision DNA: Discovering Reality Based Decision Making,* 61. Infinity Publishing.

Chapter 5

1. Friday, D., S. Ryan, R. Sridharan, and D. Collins. 2018. "Collaborative Risk Management: A Systematic Literature Review." *International Journal of Physical Distribution & Logistics Management* 48, no. 3, pp. 231–253.

2. Fan, Y. and M. Stevenson. 2018. "A Review of Supply Chain Risk Management: Definition, Theory, and Research Agenda." *International Journal of Physical Distribution & Logistics Management* 48, no. 3, pp. 205–230.

3. Manhart, P., J.K. Summers, and J. Blackhurst. 2020. "A Meta-Analytic Review of Supply Chain Risk Management: Assessing Buffering and Bridging Strategies and Firm Performance." *Journal of Supply Chain Management* 56, no. 3, pp. 66–87.

4. McShane, M. 2018. "Enterprise Risk Management: History and a Design Science Proposal." *The Journal of Risk Finance* 19, no. 2, pp. 137–153.

5. Slovic, P. 1987. "Perception of Risk." *Science* 236, no. 4799, pp. 280–285.

6. Pretz, J.E. 2008. "Intuition versus Analysis: Strategy and Experience in Complex Everyday Problem Solving." *Memory and Cognition* 36, no. 3, p. 13.

7. DuHadway, S., S. Carnovale, and V.R. Kannan. 2018. "Organizational Communication and Individual Behavior: Implications for Supply Chain Risk Management." *Journal of Supply Chain Management* 54, no. 4, pp. 3–19.

8. Mentzer, J.T., W. DeWitt, J.S. Keebler, S. Min, N.W. Nix, C.D. Smith, and Z.G. Zacharia. 2001. "Defining Supply Chain Management." *Journal of Business Logistics* 22, no. 2, pp. 1–26.

9. PMI. 2023. In *Process Groups: A Practice Guide Independent,* 340. Publisher Group.

10. Bode, C., S.M. Wagner, K.J. Petersen, and L.M. Ellram. 2011. "Understanding Responses to Supply Chain Disruptions: Insights From Information Processing and Resource Dependence Perspectives." *Academy of Management Journal* 54, no. 4, p.833.

11. Munir, M., M.S.S. Jajja, K.A. Chatha, and S. Farooq. 2020. "Supply Chain Risk Management and Operational Performance: The Enabling Role of Supply Chain Integration." *International Journal of Production Economics* 227, p. 107667.

12. Kleindorfer, P.R. and G.H. Saad. 2005. "Managing Disruption Risks in Supply Chains." *Production and Operations Management* 14, no. 1, pp. 53–68.

13. Seyedan, M. and F. Mafakheri. 2020. "Predictive Big Data Analytics for Supply Chain Demand Forecasting: Methods, Applications, and Research Opportunities." *Journal of Big Data* 7, no. 1, p. 53.

14. Günther, W.A., M.H.R. Mehrizi, M. Huysman, and F. Feldberg. 2017. "Debating Big Data: A Literature Review on Realizing Value From Big Data." *The Journal of Strategic Information Systems* 26, no. 3, pp. 191–209.

15. Maroufkhani, P., R. Wagner, W.K. Wan Ismail, M.B. Baroto, and M. Nourani. 2019. "Big Data Analytics and Firm Performance: A Systematic Review." *Information* 10, no. 7, p. 226.

16. Pournader, M., A. Kach, and S. Talluri. 2020. "A Review of the Existing and Emerging Topics in the Supply Chain Risk Management Literature." *Decision Sciences* 51, no. 4, pp. 867–919.

17. Holling, C.S. 1973. "Resilience and Stability of Ecological Systems." *Annual Review of Ecology & Systematics* 4, pp. 1–23.

18. "Supply chain resilience." September 22, 2023. Wikipedia. https://en.wikipedia.org/wiki/Supply_chain_resilience.

19. Dreyfus, H.L. and S.E. Dreyfus. 2005. "Expertise in Real World Contexts." *Organization Studies* 26, no. 5, pp. 779–792.

20. Deming, D.J. 2021. "The Growing Importance of Decision-Making on the Job." National Bureau of Economic Research Working Paper Series, Working paper No. 28733, p. 55.

21. Schuster, R., G. Nath, P. Rodriguez, C. O'Brien, B. Aylor, B. Sidopoulos, D. Weise, and B. Datta. July 29, 2021. "Real-World Supply Chain Resilience." Boston Consulting Group. www.bcg.com/publications/2021/building-resilience-strategies-to-improve-supply-chain-resilience (accessed November 20, 2023).

Chapter 6

1. Barney, J. and W. Hesterly. 2012. In *Strategic Management and Competitive Advantage*. 4th ed. Pearson.

2. Bajec, P. and I. Jakomin. 2010. "A Make-or-Buy Decision Process for Outsourcing." *Promet—Traffic & Transportation* 22, no. 4, 7. pp. 285–286.

3. Gunasekaran, A., Z. Irani, K.L. Choy, L. Filippi, and T. Papado-poulos. 2015. "Performance Measures and Metrics in Outsourcing Decisions: A Review for Research and Applications." *International Journal of Production Economics* 161, pp. 153–166.

4. Ibid, p. 154.

5. Sanders, N.R., A. Locke, C.B. Moore, and C.W. Autry. 2007. "A Multidimensional Framework for Understanding Outsourcing Arrangements." *Journal of Supply Chain Management* 43, no. 4, pp. 3–15.

6. Serrano, R.M., M.R.G. Ramírez,and J.L.G. Gascó. 2018. "Should We Make or Buy? An Update and Review." *European Research on Management and Business Economics* 24, no. 3, pp. 137–148.

7. Cappa, F., R. Oriani, E. Peruffo, and I. McCarthy. 2021. "Big Data for Creating and Capturing Value in the Digitalized Environment: Unpacking the Effects of Volume, Variety, and Veracity on Firm Performance." *Journal of Product Innovation Management* 38, no. 1, pp. 49–67.

Chapter 7

1. CAPS Research. July 2003. "CAPS Research Purchasing Performance Benchmarking Study." Managing Your Services Spend in Today's Services Economy. Tempe, AZ.

2. Delgado, M. and K.G. Mills. 2018. "The Supply Chain Economy: A New Framework for Understanding Innovation and Services." *Harvard Business School.* p. 10.

3. OCED 2023. *Gross Domestic Product (GDP) (Indicator).* https://doi.org/10.1787/4537dc58-en (accessed on May 31, 2023).

4. "World Bank National Accounts Data, and OECD National Accounts data files." 2018. The World Bank. https://data.worldbank.org/indicator/NV.SRV.TOTL.ZS (accessed on March 5, 2019).

5. Stevenson, W.J., M. Hojati, J. Cao, H. Mottaghi, and B. Bakhtiar.2021. In *Operations Management,* 7th Canadian ed. McGraw-Hill Ryerson Limited.

6. Akkermans, H. and B. Vos. 2003. "Amplification in Service Supply Chains: An Exploratory Case Study From the Telecom Industry."

Production & Operations Management 12, no. 2, p. 205, pp. 204–223.

7. PMI. 2004. A Guide to the Project Management Body of Knowledge, 371–4. 3rd ed. PMI Press.

8. Choudhury, T.T., S.K. Paul, H.F. Rahman, Z. Jia, and N. Shukla. 2020. "A Systematic Literature Review on the Service Supply Chain: Research Agenda and Future Research Directions." *Production Planning & Control* 31, no. 16, pp. 1363–1384.

9. Ellram, L.M., W.L. Tate, and C. Billington. 2004. "Understanding and Managing the Services Supply Chain." *Journal of Supply Chain Management* 40, no. 4, pp. 17–32.

10. Gunasekaran, A., Z. Irani, K.L. Choy, L. Filippi, and T. Papadopoulos. 2015. "Performance Measures and Metrics in Outsourcing Decisions: A Review for Research and Applications." *International Journal of Production Economics* 161, pp. 153–166.

11. Elgazzar, S. and S. Elzarka. 2017. "Supply Chain Management in the Service Sector: An Applied Framework." *The Business and Management Review* 8, no. 5, p. 11.

12. Croxton, K.L., S.J. Garcia-Dastugue, D.M. Lambert, and D.S. Rogers. 2001. "The Supply Chain Management Processes." *International Journal of Logistics Management* 12, no. 2, pp. 13–36.

13. Johnson, M. and C. Mena. 2008. "Supply Chain Management for Servitised Products: A Multi-Industry Case Study." *International Journal of Production Economics* 114, no. 1, p. 30, pp. 27–39.

14. Baltacioglu, T., E. Ada, M. Kaplan, O. Yurt and Y.C. Kaplan. 2007. "A New Framework for Service Supply Chains." *Service Industries Journal* 27, no. 2, pp. 105–124.

15. Selviaridis, K. and A. Norrman. 2014. "Performance-Based Contracting in Service Supply Chains: A Service Provider Risk Perspective." *Supply Chain Management* 19, no. 2, pp. 153–172.

16. PMI. 2021. In *A Guide to the Project Management Body of Knowledge and the Standard for Project Management,* 7th ed. PMI Press.

17. Weyers, M. and L. Louw. 2017. "Framework for the Classification of Service Standardisation." *Service Industries Journal* 37, no. 7–8, pp. 409–425.

Chapter 8

1. Bickel, J.E. and R.B. Bratvold. 2008. "From Uncertainty Quantification to Decision Making in the Oil and Gas Industry." *Energy Exploration & Exploitation* 26, no. 5, pp. 311–325.
2. Chenger, D. and J. Woiceshyn. 2021. "Executives' Decision Processes at the Front End of Major Projects: The Role of Context and Experience in Value Creation." *Project Management Journal* 52, no. 2, pp. 176–191.
3. Holling, C.S. 1973. "Resilience and Stability of Ecological Systems." *Annual Review of Ecology & Systematics* 4, pp. 1–23.
4. "Sustainability." n.d. United Nations. www.un.org/en/academic-impact/sustainability (accessed July 5, 2023).

About the Author

Denise Chenger, PhD, is an Associate Professor at Mount Royal University, where she instructs courses in project management, decision making, strategy, and operations. Her research interest focuses on strategic decision making and how those decisions are disseminated and executed as projects. She is currently examining the organizational changes (people and culture, process, data, and technology) required for companies implementing big data initiatives. She has been published in *Project Management Journal* and *Supply Chain Management Journal*.

Her career started in the retail industry and then moved into downstream oil and gas, working in senior-level roles in both Canada and the United States. She has led numerous business transformation initiatives in both leadership roles and as a consultant, where she has delivered tangible and value-creating results. The last decade has focused on large-scale strategic change initiatives in a variety of industries. She holds a PhD (The University of Calgary), an MSc in Project Management (University of Alaska), and an MBA from the Ivey School of Business.

Index

OTHER TITLES IN THE PORTFOLIO AND PROJECT MANAGEMENT COLLECTION

Kam Jugdev, Athabasca University, Editor

- *Project Teams, Second Edition* by Vittal S. Anantatmula
- *Lead Then Learn* by Annie MacLeod
- *Tune-Up Your Small Business* by Raewyn Sleeman
- *The Professional Project Manager* by Carsten Laugesen
- *The Agile Enterprise* by David Asch
- *A Project Sponsor's Warp-Speed Guide* by Yogi Schulz and Jocelyn Lapointe
- *Power Skills That Lead to Exceptional Performance* by Neal Whitten
- *Great Meetings Build Great Teams* by Rich Maltzman and Jim Stewart
- *When Graduation's Over, Learning Begins* by Roger Forsgren
- *Project Control Methods and Best Practices* by Yakubu Olawale
- *Managing Projects With PMBOK 7* by James Marion and Tracey Richardson
- *Shields Up* by Gregory J. Skulmoski
- *Greatness in Construction History* by Sherif Hashem
- *The Inner Building Blocks* by Abhishek Rai

Concise and Applied Business Books

The Collection listed above is one of 30 business subject collections that Business Expert Press has grown to make BEP a premiere publisher of print and digital books. Our concise and applied books are for…

- Professionals and Practitioners
- Faculty who adopt our books for courses
- Librarians who know that BEP's Digital Libraries are a unique way to offer students ebooks to download, not restricted with any digital rights management
- Executive Training Course Leaders
- Business Seminar Organizers

Business Expert Press books are for anyone who needs to dig deeper on business ideas, goals, and solutions to everyday problems. Whether one print book, one ebook, or buying a digital library of 110 ebooks, we remain the affordable and smart way to be business smart. For more information, please visit www.businessexpertpress.com, or contact sales@businessexpertpress.com.

www.ingramcontent.com/pod-product-compliance
Lightning Source LLC
Chambersburg PA
CBHW061219220326
41599CB00025B/4691